COMING OUT RIGHT

Coming Out Right

A handbook for the gay male

William Hanson and Wes Muchmore

Boston • Alyson Publications

This book is a paperback original from ALYSON PUBLICATIONS, INC., PO Box 2783, Boston, Mass. 02208. *Coming Out Right* has not previously been published in any form.

First edition, second printing, November 1983

ISBN 0 932870 21 X

Acknowledgments
While this book is entirely the responsibility of the authors, on much of its content we sought the advice and opinions of others. The following people gave very generously of their time, knowledge, and insight and have our sincere thanks: Midge Brenner, friend; R. Lyon, L.C.S.W.; Rome, San Francisco's best bartender; Leslie Alan Solomon, M.D.; Michael Walensky, friend; W.W., esq.

Contents

To Richard L.,
whose new life
inspired this book

Introduction

This handbook is intended to serve the needs of the man who is in the process of coming out, who is accepting himself as homosexual. He may be young, new to adulthood as well as to gay life, or he may be an older man who has been living as a heterosexual or in isolation.

We feel that American gay male life needs to be carefully explained for three reasons. First, the gay world is a distinct culture with its own institutions, values, and customs. Second, to the uninitiated, gay life is almost invisible. While it exists under conditions of discretion and secrecy, it is to some extent intertwined with the dominant culture, hidden in plain sight, so to speak. Finally, for the vast majority of us, nothing in our upbringing prepares us to live a gay life. Quite the contrary. Most of us have heard from childhood that gay people are loathsome and to be avoided. We are unique among minority groups in that we are raised by persons of an alien and hostile culture.

That the inexperienced gay man needs all the help he can get was made clear to us by the experiences of a friend of ours. He came out of an unsuccessful marriage, faced the truth about his sexual preference, and set out to live as a gay man. One mess followed another. We gave advice when asked, but too often we assumed that our friend understood the basics of gay life; we failed to realize that matters we took for granted were dark mysteries to him.

We looked for a book that outlined the essentials of life for the gay man in our society and found nothing suitable. Feeling that such a work was badly needed, and not only by our friend, we have put together a guide to male homosexual life, trying to make it both practical and realistic.

Our major qualification for this effort is that we are both gay men. One of us, Wes, is a writer who lives as openly gay. William is a lawyer who must still keep his gayness concealed at work. Each of us has been around for more than forty years, and between us we have a good deal of experience covering many aspects of gay life.

One problem in writing this book is that gay men have no single pattern of existence. In some areas we live and work openly. However, in most places gay people must deal with a lot of hostility and oppression. Gay men are a random selection from the whole population and can be found in all classifications of wealth, race, age, religion, talent, intelligence, occupation, and background. The gay world has its own minorities. While most homosexual men cannot be distinguished from their hetero brothers, some of us are effeminate, a few enjoy cross-dressing, and others like sadomasochism.

With all this in mind we have tried to keep our coverage broad, in order to be as widely useful as possible. We have avoided emphasis on any one region or on any single style of gay existence. Theory and speculation on the whys of homosexuality have been kept to a minimum. (Libraries are full of books that explain why men may want to love men, and the amazing variety of conclusions only indicates to us that there are no clear answers.) And we have not dealt with the problems a lesbian faces on coming out; in this we obviously lack expertise.

Though none of our friends would say that we are without strong opinions, in all that is discussed here we've tried to avoid ethical judgments. We feel it is sufficient to give information, discuss alternatives and consequences where necessary, and let the reader decide what is best for himself.

Much of the information we present is neither cheering

nor pretty. In such concentrated form it may tend to give a negative, even frightening view of gay existence. This is an unavoidable distortion. Just as a sailor would want a nautical map to draw attention to the few danger zones of a large and generally safe ocean, so too will the gay beginner want to be well forewarned of the problems he may face.

However, these problems and dangers, much as they need to be explained, do not constitute the whole of existence for gay men. A map is never a substitute for the places it represents; it only shows how to get from here to there. That is what we are trying to do, so that the transition into a new way of life can be as easy and painless as possible.

1 Coming Out

> There is nothing more difficult. . . than to take the lead in the introduction of a new order of things.
>
> — Niccoló Machiavelli

First you come out to yourself. You admit that erotically your primary interest is in other men. Many gays say that they have "always known," from earliest childhood. To others the knowledge comes as a shocking revelation, usually in their teens or early twenties. For some, after years of thinking themselves heterosexual their true orientation, having crept up on them, becomes clear at last. And there are those who know but hold out for varying periods of time as they go through the motions of a straight existence.

Occasionally a very young man will believe himself to be gay when he is not. Typically he is an adolescent who feels extremely isolated and lonely and develops intense feelings for an adult of the same sex. This sort of crush, very often on a teacher, is usually a matter of growing pains rather than true homosexuality.

Men new to their gayness sometimes believe that if they have sex with a male, or even think about it, some terrible Jekyll-Hyde change will come over them. The truth is that nothing special will happen. You will not turn into anything, develop a sudden, unconquerable yen to wear dresses, jewelry or makeup, or become a woman. You will not now lust for little boys, turn girlish, or begin to talk in a lisping manner. You will not start to hate females, lose your sense of morality, or go wild over the colors purple, lavender, pink, or green. That's all nonsense. If nobody could tell about you before, nobody can tell about you now.

Unless. . . . Occasionally when a man accepts his homosexuality he indulges impulses he has kept suppressed before. To observers this may give the appearance of a magical transformation, but almost always it represents a conscious choice.

Coming out is not always pleasant even under the best of circumstances, and it can be an extremely difficult process. Very often a man has to completely reassess and restructure his whole existence.

Along with the strains of adjustment several problems may arise from within. Difficulties frequently have two sources. First, in American society where virtually everyone is raised to be heterosexual, we all learn as children that homosexuality is a sickness or a sin. At the least we are led to view it as a faintly amusing misfortune. When a man realizes that *he* is one of *them*, a certain degree of self-hatred is almost inevitable.

Evidence of this is visible all through gay life. A man having an uninhibited weekend says he's whoring around; his partners in casual sex scenes are tricks, a dehumanizing term originally used by female prostitutes to refer to their customers. Some gay men, though gentlemanly and polite among heterosexuals, are barely civil with their own kind. Social isolation, superficial relationships, rejection of responsibility, and self-destructive patterns of life are not unknown in the gay world.

Second, many gays feel that they have had very much less than idyllic upbringings. Anyone who has grown up in an atmosphere of unusual conflict and hostility is more apt to have unresolved tensions which can affect his adult relationships. And a fair number of us have been forced to leave home before we were prepared to live on our own. This is not to say that psychological problems are the unavoidable legacy for every gay man. But the potential is there, particularly under the strains of the process of coming out.

With all the negative emotions it can raise, the discovery of oneself as gay usually brings to an end months or even years of doubts, confusion, and anguish. A dizzying sense of elation may take their place. Remember that other people in your life may find it difficult or impossible to share whatever feelings of release you may have.

Coming out to friends

Be prepared for some surprises. The friend you've regarded as the most liberal may turn out to be the one who can't handle the idea that you're gay. Others may accept it intellectually but will become uneasy when confronted by tangible evidence of your sex life, such as your lover.

Roughly speaking, your straight male friends who do not feel secure about their own sexual identification are likely to reject you.

Here you'll run into the principal difficulty faced by gay males: most heterosexual American men are homophobic; that is, they have a deep, morbid, irrational fear of homosexuals. Its expressions range from locker room jokes ("Didja hear about the fag that wore a diaphragm. . . in his throat?"), to verbal abuse, to physical assaults that sometimes end in murder. And straight males often believe a lot of folkloric silliness about gay people. Even men who by intelligence and education should know better may think that homosexuality is a disease (and possibly catching), or a form of insanity, or the result of a birth injury, or a matter of choice; that gay men routinely molest children, are united in some kind of fiendish conspiracy, and wear gowns.

Even those straight men who are not hung up about gayness may fear guilt by association if they are known to be friends with someone who is gay.

The problem is that few hetero males are self-confident sexually. Many fear their own quite normal homosexual impulses; their role stereotypes, being few and difficult to live up to, inspire self-doubts and anxiety. Thus gay men become useful to them as scapegoats and also to highlight their masculinity: "Maybe I'm not Superstud, but at least I'm no goddamned faggot."

All this said, let us point out that *some* heterosexual males will not be bothered by your sexual orientation, so don't write off *all* of them.

Straight female friends are far more likely to take your news without getting upset. You can expect a nasty reaction in only a few cases. The first, again, is the woman who is not confident of her sexuality. The men in her life all have to be possible lovers, or how can she prove she is a woman? This type is a small minority among females. The second is the woman who, although you may not know it, happens to be in love with you. Naturally she is going to be disappointed. Finally, if you've been dating a female merely to pass yourself off as Mr. Macho, she's not going to enjoy learning that she has been used.

Coming out to your family

For the young man, these are the most usual reactions:

1. Your parents will accept you as you are. This is not common, and with the best intentions in the world they may take a long time to come to terms with your situation.

2. Your parents will try to understand, but the news will make them feel guilty, as if your gayness is their fault. They probably will think your life is headed for ruin if you persist in your homosexuality, and therefore will pressure you to change. They may want you to go into psychotherapy, join the armed forces, or, if you are quite young, enroll in military school. What they don't realize is that sexual preference is extremely resistant to change by any known method of treatment, and that putting a homosexual man in an all-male environment is like locking an alcoholic in a liquor store in order to keep him out of cocktail lounges.

3. Your parents will not react. They will refuse to believe you, and the subject will never be brought up again. You may feel like an outcast, and even though life remains the same on the surface, relations with your parents can go hollow very fast.

4. Your parents will reject you. Melodramatic as this may seem, gay people do get thrown out of their family home, disowned, and told never to come back. It happens frequently, in fact.

If you are an older man, living on your own and perhaps located at some distance from your parents, you don't have the problems a younger man has — it is easier to leave well enough alone. Whatever you decide, maternal and paternal health should be taken into consideration. A bad heart and shocking news don't mix.

At any age, the parents you tell may want you to keep your gayness a dark secret. Remember, that is for you alone to decide; it's your life and nobody else's.

Brothers and sisters can be very unpredictable at any time. Homophobia, often in the form of exaggerated fears for their children's safety in your presence, or sibling rivalry, or the fear that if you are, maybe they could be, or jockeying for position in Grandpa's will, can affect their reaction. In judging this you are your own best guide.

Telling members of your family can be a way of unconsciously making matters worse for yourself rather than better. Examine your motives as carefully as you can: are you really just setting yourself up for a hard time? Are you indulging a taste for suffering and martyrdom? Might you be trying to hurt your parents in revenge for your being gay? Could you be attempting to get attention or to strengthen an unhealthy, emotionally addictive relationship to your parents? Could your announcement foment problems in their marriage?

On all sides the potential for hurt is great. Whatever you decide to do, tread very carefully and consider what is to be gained by your revelation and what lost.

Coming out at school

By and large, adolescent males are the most homophobic of straights. Any man who comes out at the average high school is much to be admired for his bravery, if not for the duller virtue of prudence.

Colleges may well foster an atmosphere of worldly tolerance that will make coming out less painful. However, if you plan a career in academia, remember that despite all the enlightenment and intelligence some faculty members will be homophobic. Others, and not a few, will be closet cases (that is, men who hide their gayness). They will not go out of their way to make life easy for anyone as unnerving as an upfront homosexual.

Coming out completely

In order to manage this successfully, it is necessary to be the son of unusually understanding parents, to live among unthreatened, sympathetic people, and to work in a situation where you are not required to project a stereotypical hetero family-man image. Otherwise, you must be very brave in the face of much hostility — verbal, physical, social, economic — or very rich.

Not coming out

In gay parlance the closet is where men who pass for straight hide their true desires. Given the ways of our society, the closet does have its advantages, and even openly gay men sometimes find it convenient to appear straight. Some closet cases manage a double life very well, wife and family none the wiser. Not every marriage is what it seems: some are composed of a gay man and a lesbian, or perhaps an understanding straight woman.

On the other hand, life in the closet with its repressions and falsifications can create great strains on one's mental health. The closeted gay man will never be supportive of other gay men or causes, and he is the first to guffaw at faggot jokes. Self-hatred is extremely difficult to avoid; indeed, choosing total secrecy is in itself a harsh judgment against one's true nature.

And there are practical problems. Exposure, such as an arrest in a toilet, can ruin a life, and blackmail can be a continual hazard. A woman who finds out she has wed a man who really thinks of her as window dressing may seek vindication in divorce court.

Sometimes a man deeply and sincerely desires not to be gay. Given the way of the world, certainly it's easier to live as a heterosexual. Various modes of therapy have been tried for changing sexual orientation, including aversion conditioning, religious conversion, and the use of medication. None of them has worked well. The successes that have been claimed often appear to be of short duration and are inconclusive as evidence: the "cures" may be borderline cases or men who merely lacked assurance with women. The difficulty may lie in the assumption that there is something to cure. Homosexuality is not a disease. It may be caused by genes or environment or trauma, some combination of these, or something else entirely. Nobody knows. It is clear only that homosexuality has been in existence throughout history and that it is practiced by some lower animals as well. Curing a man of his desire for other men may be as impossible a task as curing blue eyes of their color.

Even so, if you feel you cannot handle life as a gay man, then talk over your feelings with a therapist; he or she may be able to offer you some hope for change. Be on guard, though, against anyone from any background — medical, psychological, or religious — who promises a quick, complete transformation.

Where to come out

Valuing the friendship and warmth of straight friends and family but not wanting to live in the closet, many gay men leave their community and settle in some usually distant city that has a large gay population. New York, Chicago, New Orleans, Los Angeles, and San Francisco are common choices, and each of them has one or more gay neighborhoods or districts.

For some men this works well and gives a sense of freedom. For others, especially those with close attachments to family and straight friends, this alternative is more an exile than a liberation.

Most people would prefer the company of sympathetic souls rather than a life of isolation. However, the major gay Meccas are not unmixed blessings. Gay life often amounts to much hectic socializing and sexualizing and, on the surface at least, to little else. Some men find the gay ghetto existence with its ways of dressing, its fads and fashions, and its strong sexual competition to be extremely limiting. Others think it's heaven on Earth.

The etiquette of coming out

There are gay men that everybody can spot, that nobody can spot, and that only other gay men can spot. Some of us are upfront all the time by choice, some of us are deeply closeted, and a lot of us range somewhere in between. Every gay man has the right to decide for himself just how open he will be about his gayness, and this may vary with time, place, and situation. Among ourselves we maintain two unique courtesies.

First, you do not identify anybody as homosexual to any person who is heterosexual. This may sound like a needless warning, but it is easy to screw up, uncloseting a man who will not appreciate the favor. Example: you go to a gathering at a gay friend's place. It seems that everyone there is homosexual or straight-but-indifferent. But one of the guests may be your host's dear Aunt Minnie who dropped in unexpectedly. No matter what, you're always wiser to make no assumptions. As the phrase goes, don't let your hair down, not until you are sure that no harm will be done.

Second, in school or job situations, or anywhere else outside the gay world, homosexual men communicate information about their sexual outlook in a certain subtle way. For instance, you go on a coffee break with a guy at work, and in the course of the chitchat he mentions that last Saturday he went "to the bars." Since it's common among gay men to make the rounds of several drinking spots in an evening, the plural of the noun is a little signal. Or, he might take out a matchbook with the name of a local gay bar printed on its cover.

By these quiet means the man is telling you that he is gay and that he believes you are too. A straight man cannot respond because he won't pick up on the signal, and a gay man can choose to ignore or acknowledge it. Thus nobody is cornered, exposed, or made paranoid. This form of communication is called dropping a hairpin.

If you wish to confirm his suspicions, it won't take much to get the message to him; a wink will do. Or, referring to the matchbook (a rather obvious ploy, by the way), you need only mention that you were in that very same bar only last week. Any return signal is called picking up the hairpin.

How far to come out

Just how open you want to be is a decision to make only after carefully considering your own feelings and personal circumstances. Some men choose the closet, others refuse to hide at all, still others don't want to make a big fuss about it, and effeminate men may feel they have no choice in the matter.

Certainly for most men, the less strain and play-acting, the better. And on a larger scale, the more men who come out publicly as gay, the greater the benefit to all gay men. However many of us there are, we can't defend ourselves and maintain our rights if each of us is hiding alone. And, with the majority of homosexual males invisible, the straight world will continue to think of us in terms of the extremes rather than the means, thus reinforcing its homophobic feelings.

Many gay men combine some virtues of both discretion and openness. As must be clear by now, most straights don't want to think about homosexuality. They may know about you, but casual acceptance is another thing altogether. Many openly gay men never talk about the homosexual side of their life when they are among heterosexual friends and family. This may sound less than liberated, but often enough it is a comfortable, adequate compromise when the sure alternative is alienation from people who are very important in one's life.

However far you come out, remember that there is no reversing the situation except by leaving town and going to live among strangers. If you are in the closet now, you might want to remain there a while longer, until you are well oriented in the gay world. The information contained in this book is aimed at helping you make a decision that you can live with.

2 The Gay Bar

...all looking at their wrist watches and telling themselves: I have another hour to go — what will it bring me?
— John Horne Burns

Although many alternatives have been created in recent
years, the gay bar, for better or worse, continues as the
dominant social institution for homosexual men. Aside
from its great usefulness for meeting sex partners, the bar
often functions as a social center and source of information,
and it may provide the only sense of community, even of
family, that some gay men ever know.

Gay bars are to be found in every sizable American city,
in many smaller population centers, and at virtually any
resort or vacation area. For a man of little experience,
though, locating a suitable drinking establishment may not
be all that easy. You will understand why as we lay out the
principal means of locating a gay bar.

1. *On your own.* In some cities, such as San Francisco,
many gay places operate openly, and the action inside is
clearly visible through plate glass windows. However, this
is a new development and a break with the longstanding
tradition of anonymity that still holds in many parts of the
country. As a rule, bar owners want their business to attract
as little attention as possible. Their customers appreciate
discretion, the local police department may want such

hangouts to keep a low profile, and fag-bashers will not have a target begging for their attentions.

Look for a bar that has most or all of these characteristics:

Location: On a quiet commercial street near the main drag. Or, out on the edge of town, perhaps beyond the city limits.

Frontage: Bland, with the windows completely covered or absent; the place may even look closed.

Sign: Only one; it will be small, minimally illuminated at night. (The bar's name is likely to be quite ordinary, but even when it carries some gay double meaning, to a newly-out man the message implied by "The White Swallow," "The Ramrod," "Studio 69," or "The Basket" may not be all that clear.)

Entrance: Inconspicuous; it may even be down the side of the building. (In some few areas gay bars are customarily located on second floors.) The entry door is closed, and heavy curtains hang just inside, blocking any view of the interior from the street.

Now it should be clear why a novice may find it difficult to locate a gay bar on his own. But there are a number of other ways.

2. *The phone book.* First, check out the gay organizations in your city or nearest urban area. Look especially for a gay information line. If you can't find one, try any group that seems likely to know (not, for instance, Gay Alcoholics Anonymous). Even if it's Gay Businessmen or such, whoever answers will probably be able to help.

In some areas words like *gay* or *gay liberation* are avoided. If that seems to be the case with your yellow pages, look for listings under such words as *Homophile, Lambda, One, (Walt) Whitman.*

If you still come up empty, try calling a gay steam bath. See Chapter 3 for details. All you need say is that you are new in town and wonder if there are any nice bars around these parts. Remember that baths can be busy places on weekends, especially in the evenings, so keep it brief if you call then.

3. *Gay publications.* Many urban areas support one or more gay newspapers, some for sale and some free. These of course carry advertisements and often listings of bars, sometimes accompanied by a handy map showing where they are located. Unfortunately, these gay papers are usually found only in gay places.

And so, for the most part, are gay guides. The good ones are invaluable, listing not only the bars but also cruising places, restaurants, baths, and so forth. Several of the better known guides are listed in the bibliography as are some of the major gay periodicals, where local and national guidebooks are sure to be advertised. You may in fact be able to buy a gay guide at the local adult book store, and national gay publications can often be found at large magazine outlets.

4. *Taxi driver.* Hail a cab and ask the driver to take you to a gay bar. This can be indiscreet, even dangerous, but cabbies are accustomed to this sort of request, often take pride in knowing their city or town thoroughly, and expect that the tip will be larger than usual.

5. *The notorious hangout.* Especially in smaller cities there is one bar that everyone knows about. It's the subject of jokes among straight men and of dire warnings by fathers to teenage sons: "Don't ever go into the _____ Room. That's where the queers hang out." Typically the place has been in business for years, is located downtown, and like its neighborhood has seen better days. Its customers often include flamboyant queens, strange cases, transvestites, pillheads, and street hustlers and their mature clientele. Most denizens of such places are harmless, sometimes pathetic, but a few can be rough customers indeed.

Assuming that for the sake of information you're willing to risk being seen entering the establishment, pick a time when business is slow for your visit. Probably the early evening (6:30 to 8:00 p.m.) or the afternoon (after lunch hour until 4:00 to 5:00 p.m.) would be best. Order a beer and look around. Free local gay newspapers may be stacked on a ledge or piled on top of the cigarette machine. Behind the bar, usually near the cash register, gay guides, papers, and magazines may be offered for sale.

If there is nothing, get up, walk to the back of the bar, and look for posters advertising other drinking spots. Often these are mounted on a wall near or inside the men's room. (If a contingent of loutish-looking young men is present, and if the music is loud, then think twice about using the toilet, for whatever reason.)

Visual information lacking, ask the bartender if the place has a gay guide you can consult. Many bars keep at least one on the premises. If not, then all you can do is casually ask him about other drinking places in the area. Consider this a last resort, though. Remember, the police department has probably given this place a lot of attention over the years, and strangers asking questions may raise suspicions. The out-of-towner ploy is a dependably ordinary approach.

Cruising and drinking are the two principal activities in gay bars. Since the latter has more effect on the former than vice versa, it seems wisest to begin with boozing. (This section is aimed at young men and any others who are not experienced with alcohol; it may be skipped by others.)

Learning *how* to drink is important, and basically it means that you come to understand how to pace yourself in accordance with your capacity. A little glow can be charming, but nobody wants cold meat in bed, barf on the carpet, or another's hangover to deal with in the morning.

Drink with care at first, and keep these few things in mind. They apply widely if not quite universally:
- Pour a lot of booze down fast and you'll get sick.
- Eat sweets and drink and you'll get sick.
- Have a lot of creamy or sugary drinks or liqueurs and you'll get sick.
- Consume beer or wine after you've been drinking hard liquor and you'll get sick. The human stomach can take the shift from Schlitz to Smirnoff more easily than the other way around.

If you plan a long evening out, there is a way to slow the absorption of alcohol in your blood stream. The general idea is to have some fatty food in your belly. Before you go out you can drink a big glass of whole milk or take a teaspoon or two of olive oil. The wooziness of extended drinking can be counteracted by eating a burger or something. In any case, don't drink on an empty stomach unless you want to get very drunk very fast.

Preference usually dictates what you drink, but the various kinds of booze all have different qualities that you might consider if your preferences are not yet developed.

Beer. It's relatively inexpensive, has a manly image to it, and is all that is served in some gay bars. For these reasons it is the favored beverage of many homosexual males, particularly the younger ones. However, it is rather caloric (light beers are less so, but more watery and usually haven't much of a taste), sours the breath, and keeps the bladder busy.

Wine. A pleasure with meals, okay for an occasional glass otherwise, but definitely not to be consumed all night. The wine hangover is the worst of all possible hangovers, and what several hours' grape consumption can do to your breath is not to be mentioned in polite company. In some parts of the country wine drinking is looked on as rather sissy, and it is rarely ordered or served in S & M bars.

Hard liquor. You get less per serving than with wine or beer, but it is more potent. Clear liquors, vodka and gin mainly, have several advantages. You can drink the house brand without shuddering. They don't do much harm to the breath, and any after-effects are likely to be less painful the next day than those inspired by scotch or bourbon. These latter are preferred by men who want their booze to have a taste to it. The house or well stuff is usually drinkable but little more, so serious consumers of scotch or bourbon or other dark liquors order by brand name. These call drinks are a little more expensive than well drinks.

Liqueurs. They are not particularly popular except as an after-dinner drink or as a warmup on cold nights. The image is hardly macho, you can't drink much without getting queasy, and continuous consumption has a bad effect on your teeth and waistline.

Note that where a lot of gay bars are competing with each other the drinks are likely to be strong, possibly stiffer than in straight bars.

Liquor *is* quicker for socializing, but in the long run the best thing is to get your act together and keep it that way, rather than depend on booze to stimulate your poise and charm. In many gay bars you will find horrible examples of the disease of alcoholism. It is hard to know when social drinking gets out of control, since the progress of alcoholism is insidious. This is not to preach temperance, but to make the point that anyone who spends a lot of time in bars should be aware of the problems that alcohol can present, and should know that they can be avoided altogether.

Juicing is not taken so seriously in gay bars as it is in straight places. Gay men do not have to drink a lot in order to prove anything, and there's no loss of status for the man who doesn't drink booze at all.

If you don't like to drink, if your family is plagued with alcoholism, if you have a weight problem or diabetes, you can still enjoy the bars: try mineral water or soda with a twist of lemon or a squeeze of lime. Or order ginger ale or a soft drink.

Getting Ready

Maybe you have heard that gay men dress in some certain way. True, the gay world has its fads and fashions, but these needn't concern you right off. The basic approach is to accentuate your good points. Generally speaking, a snugly fitting pair of slacks or jeans and a nice shirt will do fine.

When to go. Bar hours reflect the rhythms of the work week, of course, but any number of variables can affect the number of customers present. Some places offer movies, raffles, and such during the week in order to build attendance on slow evenings. The suburban hotspot on Friday night may be half empty on Saturday when most of its customers, now well rested, will be barhopping in some nearby city. Whether there is a restaurant in connection with a bar can make a difference, along with many other things, like the weather, holidays, or special television programs.

If you want to check out a bar when it is fairly quiet, then the middle of the week is probably best. Many establishments open in time to catch the after-work crowd. Often there is a later group too, appearing around 9 p.m. Theoretically, then, the quietest time for a gay bar would be from 7 to 9 p.m. on a Wednesday or Thursday.

If you'd prefer to see the bar in full swing, if you like the idea of losing yourself in the crowd, the best times are usually these:

> Friday — 5-7 p.m., then 10 p.m. to midnight,
>   declining from then to closing
>   (figuring that to be 2 a.m.).
> Saturday — 10 p.m. until closing.
> Sunday — Afternoons until 7 or 8 p.m.,
>   declining thereafter.

Urban bars often are quite lively on Mondays, not only serving as an antidote to the work-week blues but also as a place to play for gay men who work on weekends (waiters, bartenders, entertainers, hospital employees, and such).

Some gay bars, especially those downtown, are open during the day, but for the first visit it's a poor time to go. The crowd in the morning consists of heavy drinkers and men who have been up all night. Around noon it's the guys who want a fast drink or two before going back to the office.

What to take. If you are young it is most important to take identification. If you are hassled elsewhere because you look underage, you will be hassled at gay bars, so bring several pieces of identification, preferably bearing your photograph.

Also bring money, but no more than you can reasonably expect to use. Otherwise, carry with you as little as you can. Your clothes look better when the pockets are flat, anyway. If you will need a credit card during the evening or plan to cash a check somewhere, don't lug a whole wallet full of plastic with you, and bring a single check rather than your checkbook.

This is not to scare you. Chances are very great that nothing unpleasant will happen, but you may be going into a not-so-hot neighborhood and might go home with a stranger, so it's a good idea not to make yourself overly tempting to the wrong kind of man.

What bars not to go to. Assuming you want a bar where you can get your bearings rather than plunge at once into the action, there are four places that probably would be of little interest to you the first time out.

The first is the dance bar. Young crowd, blasting music, verbal communication very difficult, sometimes a good deal of drug use. It might be for you, though, if you're not talkative and like to dance.

Second is the S&M bar. You will recognize it by its high tech or basement-functional decor, superstud pictures or bike club insignias on the walls, and customers in denim and black leather clothing. If you are dressed far from the prevailing macho norm, you're likely to get a little static; otherwise you will probably be ignored. Starting out at this sort of place is like tackling a Mozart concerto on your first piano lesson. But if it's what you want, see Chapter 11.

Backroom bars are sometimes of the S&M persuasion and often located in the same part of town. Simply, the place will have one or more dim chambers off the barroom where men go to have quickie sex. Socially the atmosphere isn't much, unless you really like affectless horniness.

Because of the many ordinances against cross-dressing, drag bars are few, and you're unlikely to find one by accident. And if you do, you may not discover anyone there who's in drag, though men in femme-cut pants, teased hair, eye and face makeup will be in evidence. If drag is what you're looking for, remember that transvestites often get a lot of negative reaction, so they tend to mistrust outsiders and do not respond well to even innocent curiosity. Go slow and be tactful.

You've previously been advised against the downtown toilet bar by your father and the authors both, so what is left?

What bars to go to. While bars vary in decor, location, and clientele, most of them would be suitable for a first visit. Many times gay bars are located near one another, so you may be able to check out several in one night. You can't always judge a bar by its neighborhood, though. A perfectly decent drinking place may be located in a marginal or even crummy part of the city, or it could occupy some battered old roadhouse at the edge of town. However, as far as gay bars go, you will never find a dive in a nice part of town. If you want to play it very safe, start your exploration of the bars by trying those located in the better neighborhoods.

In the bar. Eventually you will look back with amusement at your fears, but going to a gay drinking establishment for the first time often raises a great deal of anxiety. If you've imagined you'll be seized, stripped, gang-raped,and sold into white slavery, relax. The average bar contains men having a few drinks as they stand around chatting. Some may be playing billiards or pinball. And don't worry that you may meet somebody you know. You're both there for the same reason, and he could be very helpful in introducing you around.

Another fear is of raids by the police. Once common, raids into gay bars generally are on the decline and in most areas are not a real worry, though gay men in certain parts of the country may find that hard to believe. (The chapter on the police covers this, but if you should find yourself in a bar which is being raided, don't resist the officers, have identification with you, and if anything remotely weapon-like is in your hand — beer bottle, pool cue — put it down.)

Your nervous state will not be improved when you enter a gay bar. As you come through the door some men will probably turn and look at you. Then they will turn away again. You have not been snubbed, nor rejected; you've just been inspected. The best way to deal with this disconcerting action is to ignore it.

Once inside you order a drink and perhaps you will want to retire to a far corner. That's okay, but it would be better to sit at the bar, where it's easier to get acquainted. If there are a number of empty places along the bar counter, don't take the seat right next to someone. This could be interpreted as coming on with him. Sit one stool away. You or he can always move over if something promising develops.

Who is there. Besides gay men, there may be some other people present that you should know about.

In some parts of the country plainclothes detectives from the local police department's vice squad may hang out in gay bars in order to set up men for some sex offense or other. (This is dealt with in detail in Chapter 15.) If this is a problem in your area, or if you are not sure about it, follow these rules while you're in the bar:

- Hands off. Don't grope anybody, rub thighs, hold hands, play footsy or kneesies.
- If Mr. Gorgeous appears to be a stranger to the bar's patrons and employees, be careful.
- Remember that policemen often travel in pairs.
- Don't talk about sex. Don't answer any questions about what you like to do in bed. Don't say you are gay.
- It is against the law almost everywhere to indicate that a man in plain clothes is a cop. However, if while talking to Charming Stranger you notice nearby patrons looking discreetly aghast, or see that the bartender's eyes are rolling about in his head, think twice about continued involvement with this man.
- When in doubt, don't.

Some of the bar's customers may be women. This varies a good deal, with the specialized places having the fewest, and the only-bar-for-miles having a good many. Some of them may be lesbians; bars for gay women are few. Others may be straight women who enjoy the company of gay men.

Many gay bars have no females in them at all, so you may observe a unique custom, that of men using the women's restroom. This is not some weird role-reversal scene, merely practicality: with no women present, two bathrooms are available. Do not *assume* this is the practice in your area, full of beer as you may be, but don't be surprised if it is.

Last and most important, there is the bartender. He can be a good source of useful information, he preserves order, and he might introduce you to Mr. Marvelous. Unfortunately, a good bartender can be hard to find. Some bar owners feel their customers are satisfied with a pretty face and a nice body, and no matter if the kid can't remember orders, serves your drink complete with his lush thumb-

print deep inside the glass, and displays all the diplomacy of
a wounded buffalo.

Which brings us to tipping. The practice varies with
region and kind of bar, but ten percent would stand as an
absolute minimum. Twenty or more percent is not
unusual. If you plan to frequent a bar, then a certain
generosity is not a bad idea, remembering that tips are to
reward good service at present and encourage more of the
same in the future.

Making out. Whether you make the approach or somebody comes on with you, the beginning of interest is likely
to be signaled by prolonged looks, perhaps stares. (Bar
mirrors are not just decoration; they can be very useful.)
Conversation will follow. Sometimes, especially near
closing, matters can be settled with "Want to go to my
place?" But usually the negotiations are more drawn out, in
the form of apparently casual chitchat. With police
problems and a common human dislike of rejection, the
conversation is a safe, discreet way of exchanging information. Its casual level allows either party to say no to sex
without causing any hurt feelings.

Here are examples of what you should listen for and what
it really means:

"Would you like to come over for a drink?" means "Let's go
to my place and fuck."

"I'd love to ask you over, but I don't live alone" means "I
have a lover/wife/straight roommate/live with the family/
live in a crowded dorm; how about your place?"

"I have to be up a little early tomorrow, but. . . ." means
"We'll have to make it fast because I need to sleep, and I'll
have to get you up and out at dawn."

"I wish I didn't have to be up so early tomorrow" means
"I'm too tired now, but I'd really like to make it with you
soon." An exchange of phone numbers is likely to follow.

"I have a roommate, but he'll probably be asleep" means
"Don't panic if somebody else is at the apartment."

"You don't mind a house full of cats/dogs/birds, do you?"
means "Are you allergic to cats/dogs/birds?"

"My friend Don over there and I would love to have you come over for a drink" means "We're into three-way sex, how about you?"

Odd as it may seem now, all this will become very easy. Well into the conversation, usually, names will be exchanged, first names only. Remember, don't ask too many personal questions. Keep it general and casual. All the while, try to size up your new acquaintance. This is important. You may be going off with a stranger, perhaps bringing him into your house or apartment. Almost everyone you meet in a gay bar will appear pleasant, civilized, decent, and for the most part the appearance won't be dangerously far from the reality. However, the gay world is a very accepting one, and its heavy socializing can serve to put a fine polish on some very rough stones.

Is this guy known to other people in the bar, to the bartender? Does he lie or contradict himself about anything important? Can you see his jaw muscles rhythmically tighten and relax? Is he weepy, obviously drunk (however attractive), depressed, funny-eyed from drugs?

Consult your intuition as well. How are the vibes?

Hints for cruising. Two men sitting together are off limits unless they signal otherwise. If one guy introduces you to another as his lover, they're out of the game, too. Except. . . if one of the pair comes on with you over the shoulder of the other, you'll have a chance to decide if you have a taste for intrigue or not. Expect some slipping and sliding if you want to go to bed with him.

If you are not interested in action, don't come on hard. Some gay men are so habituated to flirting in bars that they do it just to keep busy. And don't tie up anybody with your attentions. The man you're chatting with may have had his parents visiting all weekend and only now has the opportunity to get laid. Give him space.

Don't be shy about moving from one seat to another; it's quite usual.

A polite refusal is all that's necessary if you are not interested in a man who is coming on. Occasionally a man who very likely has had too much to drink will become persistent. Just be firm. That usually works. If it doesn't, get a little rude.

If you are refused, take no for an answer and don't be hurt by it. Remember that the gay bar serves as a social center and drinking place; not every customer is looking for sex, and of those who are, many prefer only a certain type of partner.

If somebody buys the house a round of drinks, no more is expected from you than a nod or toast of thanks. If somebody down the bar buys only you a drink, he is interested in getting to know you better. You are obliged to do no more than thank him, but you can wander down to where he's sitting and say hello. If you find you are not interested in him, make this clear fairly soon. You can say you are just out for a few drinks tonight. After the first drink is bought for you, any further gift cocktails are assumed to signify a strengthening commitment between you and your new friend.

Needless to say, it is not too hard to hustle a few drinks and then disappear. However, it's always wise to keep a good name in a bar. Word gets around with amazing rapidity in the gay world, so it's a good idea to keep the garbage out of your act.

If you want to buy somebody a drink, it's best if it does not come as a complete surprise. A little eye contact beforehand is wise. It is considered tacky to send a drink to a guy who obviously is involved with somebody.

You can refuse a drink by setting it (unsipped, of course) at the farthest side of the bar counter, in the gutter if there is one. This is an exceedingly heavy snub and should be employed only against someone who is being terminally obnoxious toward you.

It's easy to get a thing going for the guy behind the bar, especially if you are newly out. He may in fact be the sexiest man in the place. Keep in mind, though, that he is in a profession where attractiveness and amiability count for a lot, and where a certain amount of mild flirtatiousness can bring in more tips. And the barkeep may realize you are new to all this and be a little extra nice so you'll feel comfortable.

There are other reasons not to jump to conclusions about the bartender. He may have a permanent relationship that he does not advertise in the bar. If he works a late shift he may run with a night-people crowd that only begins to wind down when most of us are getting out of bed. In short, unless you and the bartender set up a definite commitment, do not waste your time hanging around until closing. If a mutual interest does develop, he may express his in the form of one or more free drinks. In order to keep him out of hot water with the management (and sometimes the state alcohol control authorities), be sure to have a few dollars on the counter in front of you, so you at least appear to be paying. It's unwise to take advantage of his generosity, of course, and he won't appreciate it if you get sloshed. Go have coffee or a snack, and return a little before closing, if necessary. Be prepared to wait for possibly an hour after last call, and he might not be able to let you wait inside the bar. You don't look like a robber, but.... The barkeep may want to party a little, as well, before you two get to bed. Two-thirty in the morning to you is five-thirty p.m. for him.

Carding. Bars have to be careful of many laws. You may be asked for more than one piece of identification if you look underage. However, if you are required to show a lot of I.D., perhaps all of it bearing your photograph, then probably you are being discouraged from entering the bar (or bath or disco) because of your race or appearance.

Mistakes can be made, and you may look so young that three or even more pieces of identification are needed to assure the doorman that you are not underage. But if you are sure your exclusion is because of race, which is against the law, what can you do about it?

Don't make a fuss at the door. The owner of the place may call the police and claim that you are disturbing the peace. He may even have some little arrangement worked out with the men in blue.

Galling as it may be, the wisest policy is retreat. Then, if you consider it worth the time and trouble, what you have to do is try to show that your exclusion was no accident but part of a pattern. If you can find others who have been excluded on the grounds of race, you may have legal recourse.

Sometimes it isn't necessary to go to the law. Recently a gay bar in our community changed hands, and soon many complaints were made of discrimination against women and minorities. With much word of mouth publicity and little formal organization a boycott began. News of it spread by a letter-writing campaign to local gay papers, and soon the majority of the place's customers chose to stay away. Suddenly a new manager and a new policy were announced in ads that invited "ALL the gay community" to enjoy the bar.

When to stay away from the bars. If you learn that gay bars are being raided, go elsewhere. This most often occurs just before election time, when the local politicians want to appeal to the moralistic vote, and it may be all the worse if the sheriff or police chief is elected to office, not appointed.

Unless there's a party, stay away on Christmas Eve. It's a scene of sad people with no place better to go.

Stay away when you are on a huge downer. If a room full of sexy men and livening beverages won't help, don't go and drag the scene.

When you can't find a gay bar. If you live in a small town or rural area, your researches may turn up nothing at all in the immediate neighborhood. Do not despair. As you will read in the chapter on cruising places, we are everywhere.

This is the basic rule in a no-bar situation: Where the action is, there is bound to be some gay action too. What's the hottest spot around on Friday or Saturday nights? Maybe it's a piano bar, a truck stop, a steak house that brings in a three-piece band on weekends, or the bowling alley with a bar, out on the edge of town.

A distinct gay section in a bar or restaurant may exist, but it won't be obvious, especially to a newcomer to this side of life. Look for a back corner or a couple of booths where men are gathered. Otherwise, casually check out the whole place. You might pick up an extra glance from this guy, or vibes from that one. Look for such signs as a ring worn on the little finger. Many a straight wears a pinkie ring, but this can also be a signal that the wearer is gay. A newer and more definite indication is the Greek letter lambda (λ), which may be worn on a chain or as a pin.

Of course discretion is of the greatest importance, but a great deal of gay meeting and greeting goes on everywhere, right in front of totally oblivious heterosexuals.

When you leave the gay bar. Alone or with your new friend, keep an eye out for trouble. You probably won't have any, but sometimes punks intent on beating up gays will wait outside bars. The police have been known to tail men as they drive off from a gay bar, then arrest them for drunk driving. In one town, where a parking lot lay across the street from the town's lone gay bar, public records showed that virtually all citations for J-walking had been issued to single men.

These problems vary from zero to acute, and the best information that you can get about them will come from the staff of the local gay bar. Occasionally a notice is posted to warn customers of hassles in the street. Take it seriously.

The gay bar continues in its importance to gay men despite various kinds of competition that have developed in recent years. At its best it provides a great deal that's pleasant socially and sexually; finding a gay bar where you feel at home can add a great deal to your life; it's like joining a club of amiable men with interests pleasantly similar to yours. At its worst it can be unhealthy, a bad habit, and a waste of time. A great deal depends on how you make use of this gay institution.

3 The Gay Baths

> But there's no reason why sex shouldn't exist without love.
> — John Rechy

A hundred years ago, before indoor plumbing became common, the public bath house was found everywhere in the United States. Today, most baths cater to a gay male clientele. Most, but not all.

Where the baths are

If you don't have a gay guide or local gay publications, you can use the yellow pages of the phone book, but you will have to select with care. Read the entries under Baths or Health Clubs with close attention. Eliminate any ethnic establishments — Swedish, Finnish, Mexican, Russian, Jewish, whatever — it's a rare one that's not pin straight. Since the sexual revolution, in large cities an occasional steam bath operates for heterosexual men and women who want to get it on. Baths for lesbians are rarities.

Straight places usually can be identified from their display ads, but a problem may arise because the bath for businessmen and their hangovers may advertise in a manner similar to gay baths. The straight male steam bath will have most or all of these characteristics:

Long established.

Located in the older, more central part of town.

Advertises Ladies' Day.
Offers massage service, possibly also a barber shop.
Open less than twenty-four hours a day.
    The baths you want may list sundecks and saunas in their ads, movies, billiards, gymnasium equipment, and swimming pools, but will rarely offer massage. They will be open all night and emphasize that they are for men only.

When to go. The busiest times are Friday nights, Saturday afternoons and especially Saturday evenings, and Sunday afternoons. If you'd rather go when it's quiet, weekday afternoons and Sunday evenings are probably best. Weekday mornings are usually too quiet.

Who will be there. As a rough rule of thumb, if there's only one establishment in your locality, it will attract some of everybody, and if there are a number of baths, there will be a degree of differentiation in their patronage. One place may have a lot of older men, another will be very racially mixed, the young crowd will favor a third.
    Basically, the men you find in a steam bath are there because they want sex with a variety of partners. The ease of meeting brings together men who might never encounter each other anywhere else, or who might not consider the other as a pickup in the bars. A young guy might enjoy half an hour in bed with an older man where he wouldn't dream of an all-night scene. A member of a minority group may find more acceptance here than elsewhere. Gays who are traveling sometimes stay in baths rather than hotels. The highly closeted homosexual and the "straight" married man will often be found at the baths, which are less public than bars and a lot safer than cruising places.

What to expect
    The tubs, as must be clear by now, are for Just One Thing. Maybe you'll find interesting conversation, meet your true love, or renew a fading suntan, but if you go to the baths for any reason but sex, you're asking for disappointment.
    This emphatic carnality doesn't please everyone, and a number of gay men rarely or never go to gay steam baths.

How the bath works. Within the entry door you will find a box office window. Here you register by filling out a card with your name and address, just as at a hotel or motel. You may be nervous about putting down the real facts, and it is true that the card is probably accessible to the local police department and can be subpoenaed. Instances of this are rare, but if it is a public place and you don't have to show I.D. to prove you are of age, then you can fill in a false name and address. If the bath must operate as a private club, you will have to show identification in order to take out a membership. Generally speaking, no harm results from registering under your own name, but be aware of the slight risk involved.

Tell the cashier whether you want a room or a locker. The former, giving comfort and privacy, is preferable, especially on a first visit. The cashier will inform you if no rooms are available at the moment, or a sign reading "Lockers Only" will be posted in the window. Speak up now if you want a room when one is free. In some baths you pay for a room and get a locker to use while you wait. In others you have to pay for a locker and keep enough additional cash with you to pay for the room when it becomes available. Either way you will be paged on the PA system, by your locker number, never by name. "Bring your keys and clothes to the office" is the usual formula. You clean out your locker, change keys at the desk, and find your room.

Prices vary from place to place. They may differ with the day of the week and the time of day. The most popular and therefore most expensive times are weekend nights. Currently you will pay between five and fifteen dollars for a room and about half as much for a locker.

For legal safety's sake many baths operate as private men's clubs. This means you will have to take out a year's membership, for a few dollars extra, and you will receive a club card to show on future visits. Where police pressure is great, you can get into a bath only with a membership card from some other steam bath, or if you go with a friend who has already signed up.

Eight hours is the usual but not invariable time limit. If you stay longer, you may be asked to pay another whole fee, or you may be charged so much for each extra hour, but if the place is quiet you may be able to remain without further cost. Since the policy varies so widely, check with the office.

Whatever the number of hours allowed, your length of stay will be figured from the moment of entry (your card will be time-stamped) and not from the time you change from locker to room.

Now that you've paid your fee, empty your pockets. The cashier will shove a long safe deposit box through a slot. Put all your valuables into it except for a couple dollars in change. The attendant will retrieve the container and shut its lid without touching any of the contents. Then he will lock it into a safe and give you the key. With it on an elastic band or a chain will be a second key, the one to your room or locker. It will have your number on it.

You also will get a towel, and then you'll be buzzed through the door into the baths proper.

Just inside you may find a list of rules prominently displayed. If every regulation were followed ("All doors must remain shut," "No visiting in the rooms," etc.), then nobody would have any fun. During your stay be guided more by the customs you observe than the rules you read.

Find your room or locker, and memorize your number. The lockers are the same as in any gymnasium. Your room will be very small, with a bed, shelf or night table, some clothes hooks, a light, and possibly a strategically angled mirror. Check the light switch; it may be a three-way or rheostat. If you can't control the illumination to suit your taste, a glaring bulb can be dimmed by draping a cloth over it, but be careful not to start a fire.

Check the walls. Peek-freaks may have put holes in them. You can drape clothes over the larger orifices and plug smaller ones with chewing gum or bits of paper. If the walls look like Swiss cheese, ask for another room.

Undress and wrap the towel around your waist. Lock your room or locker, and put the key band around your wrist or ankle. You may want to take it off during sex, but don't lose it. Some men when showering leave their keys attached to their towels. This is not a good idea.

As you explore the halls you may find that your towel keeps slipping off. Dampen the overlapping ends; then they'll hold better.

Aside from passageways lined with cubicles you will find, varyingly, a TV room, food vending machines or maybe a little sandwich bar, swimming pool, weights room, a place to sunbathe. And there will be showers and one or more steam rooms.

Most baths have one or more rather dark chambers furnished with rug-covered benches and platforms strewn with pillows. These are commonly called orgy rooms.

Finding the action. Unless the place is pretty raunchy or it's a full-moon Saturday night, you might find little evidence of sexual activity. Rarely does any action take place in the hallways, TV room, locker or snack areas. You will find some messing-around in the steam room, but not a great deal. Many men find the heat oppressive and the surroundings uncomfortable. Remember, too, that spending more than ten minutes or so at a stretch in steam rooms can put a strain on your heart or cause dehydration and, in extreme cases, collapse.

As you wander up and down the halls you will notice that some of the cubicle doors are open. If the man within a room is lying face down, he wants to be fucked. The face-up position means he wants a blow-job. A man sitting on the bed or lying sideways is not defining his desires. Sometimes you might find a door open to reveal two (or more) men having sex. Either they have forgotten to close it or, more usually, they want others to join the party.

You will find lots of action in the orgy rooms. You can remove your towel, place it around your neck, and step into the scene. If hands or mouths or cocks are doing something to you that you don't like, push them away firmly but gently. If you want your cock sucked, sit down on a bench or platform and spread your legs. Play with yourself if you like. Your body language will be understood. And if you wish to suck cock, now you know what to look for when your eyes become accustomed to the dimness of the room.

Oral sex is most common in steam chambers and orgy rooms. Anal sex occurs more often in cubicles.

Getting some. Cruising is far less complicated than in the bars. If you see somebody attractive in the halls, use your eyes. If he's in a room, stop and nod or say a quiet hello. He may look away, signifying lack of interest, or he may beckon or ask you to come in. If he doesn't react, the formula question is, "Want some company?" He may say yes, or he may give the formula turndown, "I'm just resting."

With the man who is lying face down you probably will have to be more bold, entering the cubicle and running your hand up his thigh to his ass before he reacts to your presence.

Do not be upset by rejections. Remember that many men really are resting; they just keep the door open for air and to watch the passing parade. Even if you are Young Adonis, the man you find interesting may turn on only to elderly, beer-gutted redheads. The baths are a sea populated by many fish.

Your first visit may lead you to believe that everyone else is an erotic superhero, endlessly fucking and sucking and shooting. Sex drive varies a good deal, of course, but what you are observing is mostly an illusion. Many men save their ejaculation for their final partner. Some men don't come at all, though this is less common. Don't be surprised if the flaming sex you're having with someone comes to an end without a climax or with a faked orgasm. It's nothing personal.

You too might wish to carry on for an extended time with a series of partners. For the younger man this may seem to be an impossible feat, but all that's necessary is a little practice. Enjoy the feelings you have during sex, don't merely rush through them to the finale. Unlike piano practice, this discipline is pleasant to learn, and even when you make a mistake you still have a good time.

In the halls even a good friend may acknowledge you with the barest of nods, and somebody with whom you shared the most intimate physical relationship half an hour ago might not even see you. Don't be hurt; you are not being snubbed; it's usual and accepted in the single-minded bath scene.

Services in the baths. Baths differ considerably, but virtually all have public telephones, cigarette machines, and food. Many of them sell lubricant, poppers, combs, safety razors, prophylactics, and sometimes gay publications. Some are in vending machines, some can be bought at the office.

Fresh towels are available for a small charge. Some baths will have blankets in the cubicles; at others you can get one by asking the attendant.

If you are a doctor or otherwise need to be in contact with the outside world, the office will page you for important phone calls.

In most baths you can be awakened at a certain hour on request.

Generally, tipping is not expected, but it's not out of the question if a bath attendant does you a special service, like changing your messy sheets.

The steam bath as hotel. Some gay men like to stay in steam baths while traveling. There are some drawbacks, however. Few baths offer in-and-out privileges, and a great many of them have the stereo going all the time, often playing loud, wailing rock or loud, mushy elevator music. Some places turn the volume down or off at late hours, but many do not.

Problems

First, theft. There is little in any well-run bath, but watch your keys and keep your room locked.

Second, if you get into a sex scene that you find is too much to handle, simply voice your objection to your partner(s). Usually that is enough. If it isn't, don't resist wildly, especially if you are outweighed or outnumbered. Just say that you are turning off. Remember that resistance can be sexually exciting, and confusing as well: some guys resist as a game, signaling that they want to be "forced." But a bored attitude is almost always guaranteed to drag your partner.

If nothing serves, then yell. Bath managers hate trouble. Be assured that in most baths there is very little in the way of bad scenes. A greater problem by far is the customer who is drunk. Steam bath employees try hard to keep out anyone who is juiced, but some men can get very bombed without showing any signs, and others bring a bottle with them and get schwacked on the premises. They are little trouble unless you're in your room with the door open. If one comes in, be firm about your lack of interest. If that doesn't help, stand up as if to leave the cubicle, making sure he moves out ahead of you. Then close and lock the door on him. Wait until he goes away. If he makes a lot of racket, pay no attention; his noise will bring a member of the staff who probably will eject him.

In extreme cases, where a drunk will not leave you alone anywhere in the baths, inform the management, if possible giving the jerk's room or locker number. These instances are rare.

Prostitution. Whoring is discouraged in gay baths. In the unlikely situation where someone tries to hustle you for money after sex, don't pay. If he becomes insistent, threaten to inform the office.

If you and your partner wish to buy or sell sexual services, keep the matter strictly between yourselves, or you will be thrown out.

Dope. Many baths sell poppers (amyl nitrite, isobutyl nitrite), and customers often bring marijuana. In some localities the use of grass is more or less openly tolerated. Elsewhere it is strongly discouraged, usually because it can give the police reason to raid the place. If you aren't sure what's what in your area and you must smoke, then lock yourself in a toilet and puff the fumes out a window or a vent.

If you recall what your mother told you about taking candy from strangers, you will understand that it is not terribly wise to accept an unknown drug from an unknown person. True, it probably will mean no more than a delicious time followed by a slight headache; but, on the other hand...

Diseases. Among the minor ailments, athlete's foot can be a problem, and so can pubic lice, commonly called the crabs. Most baths dread a reputation for uncleanliness and keep the premises as sanitary as possible. They cannot, however, guarantee perfect health on the part of every customer.

A man has a case of gonorrhea (the clap) but doesn't realize it yet. If he has three sex partners at the baths, and if each of them has three other sex partners (a conservative estimate altogether), then it's possible for a dozen or more infections to come from a single source. Syphilis, though fortunately far less common, can also spread easily.

There are precautions you can take to reduce your chances of getting venereal disease no matter how often you go to the baths or how wildly you carry on while you are there. See Chapter 13 for details.

Leaving the baths. Probably you will want to take a final shower. Your skin may be somewhat dehydrated, so it might be a good idea to apply some body oil. When you are dressed, be sure you have everything, then take your keys to the office. There you will be given your card to countersign, as proof that you have received your valuables. If you signed in with a fake name, remember to use it again when you sign out.

The attendant will put the metal box into the slot so you can retrieve what you had locked up. Then you will be buzzed out the exit door.

The private club

This is a recent development, having evolved out of the back room bar. It's a cross between a steam bath and a saloon, with a little bit of Elks' lodge thrown in. Some of these places are merely labyrinths, dimly lit and full of bath-like cubicles, large orgy rooms, and sanitary facilities that feature a vast array of glory holes. Others are more elaborate and have something of a true club-like atmosphere. Members may relax and converse, read, or watch television.

Private clubs are confined to larger cities and are most easily located by checking the local gay publications, where they advertise heavily. You'll have to purchase a membership in most cases, then pay a small additional fee on each visit. Some clubs are always open, others close from dawn until afternoon or early evening. These establishments are popular for many reasons. Private clubs are less well equipped with showers and such than steam baths, but they are not as expensive. Clubs are open after the bars close. In some places a member can bring his own liquor, check it at a "bar," then have it served up as required. Patrons dress as they choose, in street clothes, fetish gear, a towel, or nothing at all. Naturally,men who like their sex heavily dosed with fantasy are attracted to private clubs, and so are devotees of public toilet cruising. For them the club can be a suitable and safe alternative.

Some private clubs cater to men whose interests center about fisting and S&M. Others are less specialized. One place may have members who go for everything that is wild, druggy, raunchy, and bizarre. Another may attract a more conventional crowd. Any private club might be a bit much for someone new to the gay world. Most steam baths are sedate in comparison.

The gay steam bath, wholeheartedly dedicated to the pleasures of masculine sexual promiscuity, is an Eden of sensuality for some. For others the ambience seems sordid, manic, and emotionally cold. Still other men find the baths to be too much of a good thing. Reactions vary, but the gay steam bath is a unique institution, with no real equivalent in the straight world. It stands as perhaps the best organized and most complete rejection of puritan values that exists in America today.

4 Cruising Places

vicesquad sex! undergound! made to sneak!
— Harold Norse

If you were to stroll down a busy city street and cruise the first fifty men coming in the opposite direction, you'd probably be surprised at how many would cruise you right back. This wholesale approach is not recommended, but it does suggest that gay men who want sex can be found in a lot of places. Some locations, though, are better than others.

Finding the action
Basically, where there are a lot of people, there will be cruising going on. There are also more private spots, some of them such that you can, if you dare, have sex there and then. Otherwise you use public cruising merely for meeting so that you and your acquaintance can arrange to have sex when and where convenient.

Gay guidebooks list cruising spots all over the country. Lacking a guide, certain places are good bets for action:
Urban and suburban areas:
   • A cafe or restaurant that is open twenty-four hours a day. (Best at night, the later the better, and especially after the bars close.)
   • Public buildings such as museums and libraries.

- Bus stations.
- Streets outside bus stations. (The more rundown the neighborhood, though, the more likely you are to find hustlers.)
- Public places such as parks, beaches, college campuses, shopping malls, amusement parks.

Small towns and rural areas:

- Truck stops, especially where major highways cross. Since as a rule they are open twenty-four hours a day, action is possible at any time, though night is probably best. (A CB radio code for gay men, by the way, is "three-legged beaver.")
- Weigh-in scales for trucks. (If there's activity, it will occur after the facility is closed for the day.)
- Rest stops.

Certain facilities need a little explaining. Not all public toilets are tea rooms; that is, some restrooms serve only their obvious purpose while others are used for sex too. These latter are favored because they are not too public. It's the facility on the far, wooded side of the park that is most likely to be a tea room. Every college campus (well, except in all-female schools) seems to have one, often in some quiet basement or lightly traveled third floor. Department store men's rooms are frequently popular because they're hidden away, back of partitions and behind elevator shafts.

In the ordinary restroom men relieve themselves and leave at once. The tea room has loiterers. You can also spot a place which is sexually popular by the nature of the graffiti on its walls and by the glory holes carved through the panels of the toilet stalls.

Sex goes on between men in the balconies of certain movie theaters. A typical setting would be a huge old barn of a place in a declining downtown neighborhood. It's a weekday afternoon, the film is a real dog, there's hardly a soul on the main floor, but quite a few men are sitting upstairs. They shift their seats from time to time, and despite the lovely summer weather outside, many of them have brought an overcoat or a raincoat. Yes, you've found a cruisy movie house.

Film theaters that show gay male pornographic movies often have a back room or a spacious men's room. Most of these operate as private clubs, so you have to buy a year's membership for a few dollars.

Adult book stores sometimes have dirty-movie booths in an alcove; a certain amount of action may be tolerated there. Gay dirty book stores are usually not very good for cruising, strange to say; perhaps the books and magazines provide too much competition for mere reality.

Anyone who hitchhikes much is bound to get propositioned, and in some rural areas there are certain stretches of highway where thumbing a ride is really a means of meeting a sex partner. In a few cities, notably Los Angeles, men cruise each other from car to car. Consult a gay guide or a friend for the word on any local automobile-related action.

Making out

Generally speaking, eye contact is where you start. That may be all you need to get someone to follow you out of the truck stop and into the bushes. Conversation will be necessary, though, if there's no immediate prospect of having sex, as when you are cruising museums, shopping malls, and other very public places.

Here is how to get to the point of chitchat with an intended sex partner: as you walk along, on seeing an interesting man you fix your eyes on his as he approaches. (If you're shy, look at his forehead; the effect will be the same.) Be ready to turn your gaze away at once should you sense that he does not appreciate your attentions. If the guy looks back steadily, chances are good that he wants to know you better. After you and he pass each other, keep walking a ways, then stop casually to check out a window display, rack of merchandise, painting, whatever. Now take a look in the direction of your quarry. Has he too decided to halt and examine something or other? Is he looking at you from time to time? If so, the next step is to get acquainted. Depending on the situation, there may be more cat-and-mouse game, but an approach is in the offing. You do not go up to the man, nor does he come to you. One of you happens to wander over to examine what the other is looking at.

One of you starts talking. Any neutral little comment will do: "Nice jacket" or "Nice painting." Just remember that the really hopeless cliches, asking for a match or the time, have a rather vice-squaddy ring to them.

From here on, just as in bar conversation but in more discreet and compact form, all that's said will carry useful information about the possibility of getting together.

While this sort of cruising varies with the situation, its essence remains the same: discretion. You don't do anything out of the ordinary, you don't attract undue attention.

In toilets the communication is by body language and gestures rather than speech, as a rule. Men stand at the urinals and play with their cocks. One may lean back slightly to show himself to another. They may go on to fondling each other's genitals, and one may end up sucking off the other. The guys sitting in the stalls usually want to suck cock, and a man who wants to be sucked can enter the stall or he can take the next one and make use of a glory hole in the partition.

Communication is by touch in movie theaters. One man sits down next to another and after a brief time he gropes the other guy's crotch. (The flies of both men are probably open.) Then, when it seems appropriate, he will suck the man's cock. Afterwards, as a rule, he will leave again, moving to some other seat. Sometimes the action is mutual, but very often it's a one-way scene.

The man who wants sex with a hitchhiker he has picked up will make his desires known pretty fast, especially when he's merely cruising the outskirts of town. If the rider is not interested, the driver will say something like, "Well, this is where I turn off," and deposit the rider on the highway at a crossroads a few blocks from where he picked him up.

Problems

This cannot be emphasized too strongly: PUBLIC CRUISING CAN BE EXTREMELY DANGEROUS.

While a pickup in a shopping mall can be done with a

good deal of discretion and may have only pleasant consequences, the dangers rise considerably when you have sex with someone in public toilets, park shrubbery, or the like. With any kind of cruising there is always the chance that you may hit on the handsomest man on the vice squad, of course, but public sex exposes you to the ire of homophobic young men as well.

Precautions. If you "just can't stay away" or if you live where there are no alternatives, you're going to have to be careful.

It's a good general rule that the better known a cruising place is, the more dangerous it is. After the police become aware of it the news may go no further, but if you hear members of the heterosexual general public snickering about such-and-such Park or wherever, then be sure to stay away. The place is *hot.*

Remember that vice cleanups look especially good in the newpapers just before elections.

Pay attention to gossip. If you hear of raids in the planning stage, maybe it's just the expression of some gay man's paranoid feelings. But word of mouth is important among homosexual men, and some quiet guy clerking at police headquarters may have passed the news to others on the basis of good information.

Do not become too secure. True, most heterosexuals don't know what to look for as far as gay cruising goes, so they see nothing. Two men chatting at a store window, so what? You can begin to feel invisible after a while, sexually speaking, and this can lead you to drop your guard.

College students should be aware that the campus tea room often is raided during the first week or two of school, the idea being to discourage its use for the rest of the term.

Department store managements strongly discourage men's room sex on their premises, often going so far as to hire security forces to make arrests.

In his book *The Gay Mystique*, Peter Fischer writes, "...there is something self-serving about those straights who criticize gay people for meeting in unconventional places while making it hard for them to meet anywhere else." True, but more than social pressure is involved. Despite the considerable legal hassles, the lack of physical safety, the discomforts, and the growing number of alternative ways to meet men, the more dangerous kinds of public cruising continue to be popular. For some, a sense of peril adds excitement. For others, sex and bodily functions are erotically linked. Certain men can enjoy sex only in situations they can see as dirty or degrading. And there are those who unconsciously wish to be caught in the act and punished.

Sex in public may not be your thing, but a lot of men like it, so at some time or other you may be tempted to mess around in some unusual location. Whether you carry on in this way often or rarely, please remember the ancient saying:

If you can't be good, be careful.

5 Male Prostitutes

or if he had seen in a shop window and craved
some beautiful blue shirt,
he would sell his body for a dollar or two.

> — C. P. Cavafy
> (Rae Dalven translation)

The world's oldest profession is by no means limited to heterosexuals. There's plenty of gay male love for sale. Let's start with the best-known.

Street hustlers. These young men stand about on certain corners of a city, usually in some rundown neighborhood, or they may stroll up one side of a street, always in the same direction as automobile traffic, and after a few blocks return down the other side. They may be found in certain bars but most gay drinking places do not allow hustling.

Some of these guys are runaways, too young to get any other kind of work. Others, men in their twenties and thirties, have lived this way for years. At any age, most of them are no angels. Hustling at this level rarely provides a steady, decent income. Some hustlers raise extra cash by smalltime drug dealing, drunk-rolling, theft, or robbery. Street life is tough, and drug use is common.

Most street hustlers tell themselves and the world that they're straight and only have sex with men for money. This may be true in some cases, especially among runaways, but it's doubtful otherwise, especially when you consider that even a lousy regular job allows a man to lead a much easier life than does street hustling.

Troubled by definitions of masculinity and by cash-flow problems, product of a tough life from the start, often both homosexual and homophobic, the street hustler can be dangerous. He can also, when underage, get his customer into a good deal of trouble in any encounter with the police.

Keep your personal safety in mind always if you decide to pick up a hustler off the streets. This is done in the way described in Chapter 4: catching his eye, sauntering on to a shop window, saying hello. Then it is customary to suggest that you two get a beer somewhere. In some nearby bar price, place, and action can be quietly discussed. He may name a rather high fee, but bargaining is usual.

Alternatively, in some cities the hustler will come to the window of your automobile, and you can settle matters while driving around the block. If it doesn't work out, it's usual to leave the guy off where you picked him up. Or, where police pressure is not great, the hustler will do his dealing with you right on the street.

The hustler will know of a hotel with cheap rooms. This is always better than taking him to your place or his.

You should make your expectations clear when you settle on the fee. All street hustlers, it seems, like to think they are trade; that is, they remain totally passive, allowing the customer only to suck them off. A young, gorgeous, macho few indeed can operate in this fashion; most guys will do what you want as long as the money is right. But since some do limit their activities in bed, your wants should be discussed beforehand.

The hustler will of course want his money before any action occurs, but do not pay him until the last moment; at bedside when he is undressed is ideal. If you give him his fee in the bar, he may excuse himself to go to the men's room and not be seen again.

While guys who work the streets can get rough with their customers, their situation offers the coldhearted, unscrupulous man many opportunities for exploitation. There is no use being suckered by street hustlers, but neither do you have to make their lives any more difficult than they already are. Often some shivering adolescent can be had for almost nothing when it's a cold and/or rainy night, but the few dollars difference will mean a lot more to him than to you. And instead of buying a guy a drink, if he looks like he could use a sandwich offer him that instead; it'll cost about the same.

In many cities there is a better class of hustler. Neatly dressed, perhaps in coat and tie, he may be found allegedly waiting for a bus at the stop nearest to the first-class hotel; or he may be inside, nursing a drink at the bar. Very often he is a college student and does not hustle on a regular basis. He will be more expensive and possibly also more choosy than the usual street hustler. He prefers not to bargain, but chances are he will. Crudeness in your come-on will not be appreciated, though he does like a quiet frankness in business matters. Sometimes he will be working in a posh gay bar, and if so he probably wants nobody to know what he is doing, lest he be barred from the place.

Masseurs, models, escorts. These are three legitimate occupations, to be sure, but they are three euphemisms for hustlers as well. The classified sections of many gay publications and even some daily newspapers list many suppliers of these services. Some ads are placed by individuals and others by agencies (another euphemism) that have a string of young men to offer. Either way, prices are higher than in the street and usually not subject to bargaining. Special wants can be met and arrangements settled with one phone call. Some ads will mention *in* or *out*. This indicates whether the hustler will come to your place (*out*), or whether you can go to his place (*in*); the latter is less usual.

Generally speaking these men will be better for looks, education, and physique than their brothers on the street, and they rarely have crime in mind. They are businessmen of the body, pursuing the usual retail interests of high volume and rapid turnover. This can mean that the "masseur" of your choice may not be exactly rampant with steaming passion when he gets to your hotel room.

Agencies. While some, as above, are little more than message services, a few in each city run quite elaborate operations. You make an appointment (and your financial standing probably is quietly checked out beforehand), and you discuss your basic sexual likes with a tactful interviewer. He then gives you one or more binders full of revealing photographs of available young men. You choose from this selection whichever stunning youth you like. Discretion is great, the hustlers are the top of the line, and prices are very high.

Whorehouses and hotels. The bordello on the heterosexual model ("Company, girls!") is not common in the gay world, but in some slum areas there may be one or more old hotels where hustlers rent rooms. The door is left open, the guy reclines on the bed, and potential customers wander up and down the halls. These are the same hustlers who work the streets, so trouble is common, and trouble brings the police.

Advanced years, an unsocial nature, or gross physical unattractiveness may leave a man no recourse but to pay for sex. Hustlers may be sought out for other reasons as well: some gay men are fascinated with the world of the male prostitute. Others have exceedingly specialized desires and can only fulfill them by hiring a partner.

The man who is newly out in all probability fits none of these categories and in most cases would prefer to have his experiences with nonprofessionals. However, prostitution is a resource widely available in the gay world as well as in the straight scene.

6 New Alternatives

Seek not, my soul, the life of the immortals, but enjoy to the full the resources that are within thy reach.

— Pindar

Stimulated by the movements for gay pride and gay rights, recent years have seen a great flowering of alternatives to the bars, the baths, and the bushes. While most of these have sprung up in large cities and university towns, nowadays even smaller population centers may have a good deal to offer, either as complements to or substitutes for the old standbys of gay social life.

The great source for gay associations probably is the gay underground that once existed everywhere and still functions in areas where discretion must be high or the population density is low. Sinister as this "underground" may sound, it merely means that homosexual men (and women) quietly entertain their gay friends in private. A dinner invitation, or being asked to come to a discussion group, may be all that it takes to find this otherwise invisible social scene. New blood usually gets a warm welcome.

The open, formalized version of this sort of gathering is the rap group. Most large and not-so-large cities have one or more of them. Generally gay raps meet once a week, often in a church assembly room or the like. Socializing is high, the ambience is friendly and unthreatening. While a wide variety of men may attend, the rap is especially popular with guys who are just coming out.

Raps are loosely structured and may differ from place to place, but the usual pattern is this: it's punch and cookies and socializing for openers, then a brief business meeting. After that a specific discussion topic is announced, or maybe several, if there are enough participants for multiple groups. After an hour or two of rapping the evening ends with more socializing.

The warmth and charm of gay raps sometimes is slightly clouded by a problem inevitable with all kinds of discussion groups: the bores go on and on, and the people who appear interesting just sit there.

Most but not all raps are run in connection with counseling centers, where you can learn about rentals, jobs, therapy, etc. And raps generally are supported by pass-the-hat contributions.

Some cities have gay coffee houses, often church-sponsored, for men who are too young for bars or who don't care for them.

Interest groups abound where there is sufficient concentration of population, and you may be surprised at their variety. For instance, universities usually have one or more gay student organizations. There are associations of professors.

Professional groups include those for doctors, nurses, dentists, public health workers, psychiatrists and psychologists, social workers, lawyers, scientists, librarians, and journalists, to name a few.

Most large cities have an association of gay businesses.

Some gay men band together around religious beliefs: Dignity is the name of the Catholic group, Episcopalians have theirs, called Integrity, and some gay Mormons have formed Affirmation. Locally and internationally there are organizations of gay Lutherans, Presbyterians, Friends (Quakers), Unitarians, Baptists, and Jews. The Metropolitan Community Church, of the relaxed-Protestant persuasion, is specifically gay-oriented.

And if religion is definitely not your thing, you may be interested in a gay atheist league.

If you are a gay husband in a straight marriage, there is an organization for you, as there are for gay fathers and even for parents of gays.

There are clubs and societies of gays who are black, Asian, Hispanic, and American Indian. Interracial groups exist too.

Gay communes exist, as do musical aggregations, choruses, theater groups, ACLU branches, political clubs, labor unions, jogging clubs, organizations of railroad buffs, and leagues for bowling, wrestling, and baseball. There are gay Alcoholics Anonymous meetings, local gay publications that may need volunteers, and groups for the blind, the deaf, and the disabled.

Most gay organizations advertise their existence in one or more of the usual sources — guidebooks, posters in bars, gay hotlines, switchboards and events tapes, or in gay publications, frequently in the classified advertising section.

Speaking of the classifieds, they can be useful for making contact with other gay men on a one-to-one basis. They are especially handy for locating kindred souls who live in the same rural or lightly populated area. And men who are unusual in some way, or want the unusual in sex partners, make their search less difficult by placing ads.

This method does have its disadvantages. It's a slow way to meet people; not every ad would stand up in court as the whole truth and nothing but; and the classifieds can be used by bad guys as well as good guys.

Personal ads appear in many national and local gay papers and magazines and sometimes in general publications as well, usually of the literary-intellectual type. A number of magazines are devoted solely to gay-male personals. Generally, for a given fee one gets both a subscription and the opportunity to place an ad, and often mail-forwarding service too. Some mailing clubs accept any kind of classified, but most of them limit membership by age or sexual interest. They advertise in the classified sections of national gay publications. While most of these ad magazines are legitimate and some are even non-profit, a few are ripoffs.

Personal ads tend to be pretty frank, but often they're

couched in heavily abbreviated language. These are some of the more mysterious examples of shorthand in common use:

ac — active
aroma — poppers (amyl nitrite)
BB — bodybuilder
B/D — bondage and discipline
B/M, BM — black male
bottom — passive in anal sex; masochist; submissive
brn/brn — refers to eye color/hair color
C/B — cock and balls
cut — circumcised
endowed, endw, endowment — refers to penis size
FF — fistfucking
FFA — Fistfuckers of America; fistfucking
Fr — French love (cocksucking)
golden shower — urine
Gr — Greek love (anal sex)
hg, hng — hung
j/o — jack off (mutual masturbation)
limits — "respect limits" means the S will not go beyond what the M can take; "expand limits" means the S will take the M further than he has gone so far.
M — masochist; passive
MS — masochist and sadist, prefers to take former role
pas — passive
ph/ph — telephone number and photograph
recycling — drinking urine
revealing pic — frontal nude photograph
S — sadist; active
scat — feces
SM — sadist and masochist, prefers to take former role
smoke — use of marijuana
tight — refers to condition of anus
top — active in anal sex; sadist; dominant
toys — equipment useful in sex, usually dildoes, vibrators, restraints
uncut — not circumcised
vers/versatile — takes active and passive roles in sex; anything goes

W/M, WM — white male
WS — water sports, i.e. urine, enemas
yg, yng — young

The new alternatives require people in order to exist and to grow. Don't be shy about joining a group or participating in an activity that you enjoy. Nowadays isolation is not necessary, and it has never been healthy, informative, or fun. And if your kind of organization doesn't exist where you live, think about starting one. Social, political, religious, whatever, all you need do is make some phone calls and perhaps post a few announcements. There's no need to be lonely or to spend all your time in the bars.

7 First Experience

New thresholds, new anatomies!
    — Hart Crane

Although many readers will have had a certain number of sexual encounters already, gay or straight, for the sake of complete coverage let's assume that your experience has been limited.

For your introduction to gay sex try to find a partner who is experienced and considerate, then arrange a secure and comfortable place, and have plenty of time.

Avoid a quicky in the bushes or a public toilet. You'll get off, if you're lucky, but that's about all. Group or kinky sex is not a very good idea either. Early erotic experiences can occasionally have an imprinting effect, leaving behind the desire to repeat that first time again and again. Usually this is harmless, but it can be limiting. One friend had his first sex in a shower, and now he is not really happy, erotically speaking, unless he's making love under the spray.

Generally, this is what happens: sex is likely to start on the living room couch with embracings, kisses, caresses. Belt, buttons, zippers are often undone, and there may be some cocksucking. After a certain amount of heat is generated, and when clothing becomes a serious hindrance to further activity, the host suggests a retirement to the bed.

Once naked and in the sack, the partners caress and

explore each other's bodies, probably pretty vigorously, and from here on any number of things can be tried. While it might be useful to consult a gay sex manual for pointers (several good ones are listed in the bibliography), it is easy to learn about sex by doing it. Even so, here are some basics that it helps to know from the start.

Response to touch

All the body is sensuous, not merely the genitals, but certain areas are especially sensitive. Individuals vary greatly, but in general these body zones are the most likely to pay off in pleasurable sensations:

Lips — They may respond well to finger touch and to exploration of different parts of the partner's body.

Nipples — Partly constructed of erectile tissue, like the penis, they get hard during sex. Most men's nipples are highly sensitive.

Armpits — Firm manual exploration often produces something much nicer than just a tickled feeling.

Thighs — They may be very responsive on the insides, especially higher up, and so may be the line where leg meets abdomen.

Buttocks — Their inner sides, the crack of the ass up to and including the base of the spine, and the anus (especially) are all worth exploring.

Perineum — This is the area bounded by thighs, balls, and ass and is where the base of the penis is buried. Firm, rhythmical finger pressure can do wonders.

As you've probably noticed, your sex organs are not uniformly sensitive. The head of the penis is more so than the shaft, and the frenum, the dab of flesh beneath the opening, a kind of bridge from head to shaft, is the most sensitive part of all.

Uncircumcised cock heads tend to be a lot more responsive than those that are circumcised, so uncut men may have to work harder at holding back ejaculation than those who have lost their foreskins.

Scrotal skin gives pleasure especially when it is stimulated by firm but light touch. Balls can be played with quite vigorously as long as they are fondled, not squeezed.

Fellatio

Better known as cocksucking, this is one of the chief pleasures of gay men. There is no one way to do it, but the basic idea is to stimulate the erect penis with warmth, pressure, and friction by using your lips, tongue and throat. (The latter takes practice, though.) It's necessary to be careful with the teeth, and it's wise to get all chipped or otherwise sharp teeth smoothed out by a dentist.

Small bits of bridgework should be taken out beforehand, but dental plates should present no problem as long as they are firmly anchored. Be aware that a very superior blowjob can be given when uppers and lowers have been removed from the mouth. It's necessary to develop a magician-like finesse in extracting and replacing the choppers, but it may well be worth the trouble in terms of popularity.

When you are getting sucked and it's not right for you, gently state your preference if you want your partner to go lighter or heavier. It's rare that anybody's feelings are hurt.

A healthy man's semen is harmless; it's safe and customary to swallow it.

Whether you are sucking or being sucked, or doing both at once (sixty-nine), you're sure to be good at fellatio if you always remember to follow the Golden Rule.

Anal intercourse

Getting fucked for the first time is not often completely pleasurable, but men who like it, and there are many, discover that it improves a lot with only a little practice. Doing the fucking is always easier, first time or last, and many find it a great thrill.

On the bottom. It's wise, though not absolutely necessary, to clear your bowels beforehand. Some men like to douche with warm water, but this is not required. Your partner should know what he's doing, and you should have a towel and plenty of lubricant within reach.

Numerous positions are good for anal intercourse, but for the first-timer face down on the bed is probably best, or kneeling on hands and knees. Face-up with your legs on your partner's shoulders may be uncomfortable if you are not used to it, but the anal opening is spread a little more in this position than others, which is helpful, and with a pillow behind your head you can watch a lot of the action.

The anus, unlike the vagina, has little or nothing in the way of natural lubrication. Be sure you use a lubricant and be sure that your partner puts some on his cock.

Now he will ease it into you, and there is very likely to be some pain. Some of it is a matter of physiology, and the rest probably stems from personal hangups about this mode of intercourse. The best thing to do is be as relaxed as possible. It might help to have a few drinks beforehand, and a good deal of gently stimulating anal foreplay, if you are very nervous. As your partner moves himself in and out, the best thing for you to do is concentrate on not being anally uptight. You may be struck by a sudden need to defecate. Force your mind to ignore the signal; it's a false alarm. This sensation should ease up if you fight it, and after some experience it will disappear forever.

Try to sense pleasurable feelings; they're there, though obscured by others. Sometimes you will suddenly be flooded by a deeply good sensation, so good that it may strike you as an overwhelmingly rich assault on your nervous system. Much as you may want to fight it, go with it as far as you can; the rewards may be great.

Many men do not ejaculate when they are getting fucked. They get enough pleasure without having to come. Getting off can compete with the sensations in the anal area, and many men are unable to shoot while others do not remain hard throughout the act.

If you want to come, it's easiest of course when you are in the face-up position, where you can stimulate yourself most easily. It's often difficult for novices, but keep it in mind for the future.

As your partner withdraws at the end of this sex act, clamp your anus closed. Leakage is not very likely, and your friend can use a towel to minimize any mess, but you may expel some gas. It will be mostly air introduced during the recent activity, but it hardly adds a romantic touch to the occasion.

Both of you will probably want to take turns in the bathroom. You may find a few specks of blood on the toilet paper. This is nothing to worry about unless bleeding persists or in the unlikely case that you develop any signs of infection — fever, pus, sense of heat or a warm, throbbing sensation. But if you do, get medical attention at once.

On the top. Letting your partner choose the position he prefers, lubricate him and yourself. The looser his anus feels to your exploring finger, the less lubricant he will require. Some experienced men prefer to lubricate themselves. Let them do it; very often they will use less lube than you would politely apply. (Roughly speaking, the more friction, the more fun.)

If a man is tight, take time to gently finger-fuck him before proceeding, so that the pleasant sensations will help the anus to be more relaxed. Be careful not to scratch the mucosal lining within. The nail on your exploring finger should be trimmed down and smoothed.

Most men, not just newcomers, enjoy digital foreplay, and once your finger is inside you can give your partner a lot of good feelings by gently stroking the vicinity of the prostate gland. This is how you find it: with your finger well inside, align it parallel to the crack of your partner's ass, or to an imaginary line running down the middle of his body; curl the finger slowly toward the base of his cock until you feel a more or less solid bump. Stroke it with care, noting well your partner's reaction, or you may make him come before he wants to.

As you extract your finger, watch to see if the rectal flesh sticks or pulls a lot; if so, apply more lubricant.

By this time you may very much want to get it on, but do not jump onto your partner and jam yourself into him. This could occasionally cause injury, and it isn't difficult to make the anal sphincter go into spasm. The muscular ring at the entry can tighten so much that penetration becomes difficult or impossible and extremely painful.

Push inward with your cock, slowly and steadily. When the head of it moves beyond the sphincter, you will feel a breakthrough, but keep going inward at the same pace. The more experience your partner has, the more likely that he'll appreciate variety in your rhythms and a leisurely pace.

After you finish, pull out smoothly and slowly. However, when your partner is really hurting, a fast exit, as long as it is in a straight-line trajectory, may be an act of mercy.

A note on fisting. Also called fistfucking or handballing, this is the practice of inserting the hand into the rectum. It has gone from the status of tantric yoga esoterica to a fairly common activity. The gay man new to the scene is rarely interested in it, but we mention fisting here because it is easy to meet a more experienced man who likes it. There are three main problems. First and foremost, as far as nerve-ending sex thrills go, this gross molestation of the prostate gland is the end of the line. Second, this diversion is distinctly dangerous physically (see the S&M discussion in Chapter 11). And finally, with repetition a loss of muscle tone is usual. This means that the ass can end up good for nothing else, sexually speaking, and that there can be problems with retaining feces.

We feel you should think twice before you indulge in grand finales at the start of your gay sex life. If you are determined to try fisting, however, be sure to learn the techniques of giving it and taking it from a skilful practitioner. Don't try this out with some friend who's merely in an experimental mood.

Cock size. This is a nearly universal hangup and an ageless fetish as well. If you judge by the conversation among some gay men, everyone in the world has a big penis or a little one. Where are all the in-between cocks? Nowhere, in Fetishland. Reality is a better place: most men, gay or not, do not have huge penises, and most do not have tiny ones either. Whatever their length or width, all cocks function the same way, and the pleasure gained by their use is the same in everyone.

You may see advertisements for devices or substances that are alleged to enlarge the penis. The vacuum pump gizmos may loosen the top layers of skin somewhat but nothing more. Creams, pills, herbs, and potions will do nothing except waste your money.

A straight female friend once said that in her experience (which was monumentally vast, to put it mildly) her dullest lovers were guys under twenty-five who thought themselves well hung. "They think the dick does it all."

In short (no pun intended), for men who learn to be good in bed, cock size should be no problem.

Problems

Maybe you feel shy. You might be very hot but also a slow start. You may, especially if quite young, ejaculate very quickly. Don't get all worried. Experienced gay men have all had an occasional no-show or other difficulty, and your partner probably will make you feel at ease and then you'll get quite excited. And if you shoot fast, no real problem, since you'll probably be hot again very soon.

The main thing to remember is that you are not Superman and nobody else is either.

Impotence. True impotence is not common, but it isn't unusual for a man to have an imperfect scene or two in bed and then become panicky. Typically he develops a great deal of anxiety. This drives a man to go out and prove he is functional. He then fails again and feels worse. The basic thing to remember is this: sex is a pleasure, not an obligation. The best way to deal with this kind of problem is to avoid having sex until you are dying for it, and then only make it with someone you really desire.

There should be no further difficulties. However, if you continue to have problems, consider such matters as your alcohol intake and, especially in the older man, whatever medications you are taking. (Blood pressure drugs are especially villainous in this area.) Prolonged exposure to certain chemicals and to lead can cause physical impotence, but such exposure is unusual.

Should difficulties continue, do not be embarrassed: go see a doctor or a therapist. The problem may be surprisingly easy to clear up.

General cautions. When you have sex with someone who is essentially a stranger, and possibly in an unfamiliar part of town, keep these things in mind: know where you are, and know how to get home from there. Have money for a taxi or bus if necessary. It is okay to get it clear before you go home with somebody whether you can stay the night or not.

It's a good idea to keep all your clothes and possessions in one place so that you don't forget anything when you leave.

Do not be vague about what you will and won't do in sex. "I really shouldn't" will likely be interpreted as signaling that you like to be forced, and your partner may act accordingly. A yes or a no is the best answer. "I haven't done that before, but I'd sure like to try it" is a good way to clue your partner to go easy as he introduces you to something new.

Do not ever, under any circumstances, allow yourself to be tied up, handcuffed, chained, or in any other way immobilized by a stranger. Bondage is sexy and interesting for numerous people, but before you get into that scene, *know your man.*

If you have a lot of guys coming over to your place for sex, put the Really Good Stuff out of sight. You might not miss those gold cufflinks for months. And don't let a casual pickup stay alone in your place after you go off to work.

As host

Have these things within easy reach of the bed: ash tray, one or more trick towels, and lubricant. If your mattress is ancient and its central concavity fits you fine, well, consider that you are having guests in your bed and that their comfort has its importance, too. Don't forget the lighting. Most gay men don't like to make love in total darkness. Candles are nice. You can buy a dimmer switch inexpensively and install it to control the overhead light. A source of music may be a good idea, but some men find it distracting during sex, and commercials can be fatal to high erotic moods.

Avoid having to leave your acquaintance alone while you run about the house doing little errands. Have the place ready before you go out for the evening. That means dealing with pets, too. If your German shepherd has a habit of lunging at the throats of strangers, you will want to be sure the animal is out of the way when you bring home Mr. Hot.

Lubricants. Something to smooth the way is necessary for anal intercourse and often desirable for other kinds of sex. Spit is handy, but sometimes it can be too thin for the job, and the supply is always variable.

Petroleum jelly products are not as popular as legend has it. They tend to be usefully thick, but also hard to wash off, and thus possibly can harbor germs, bacteria, etc. And, with prolonged use in anal sex, any grease made from a mineral oil base could be the cause of benign tumors in the rectum.

Far more popular are the greaseless lubricants such as K-Y. These clear jellies are nearly odorless, not expensive, and come in handy squeeze-tubes of various sizes. They dry out fairly fast, but can be brought back to life with a little saliva.

As advertised in gay publications, numerous commercial lubes are available. They are made from various combinations of vegetable oils, work well and smell good, but they tend to be a little expensive.

You do not need a specially made product. Some men swear by one or another brand of greaseless hand lotion; others prefer cold cream. Crisco has its fans, mostly among the fisting crowd, but it has a heavy odor, and is not easy to remove from sheets and towels.

The best thing to do is to shop around and find out what suits you best. Avoid products with alcohol in them (like Corn Husker's Lotion), because it's there to evaporate and leave the substance dry. And remember, vegetable oils are okay, mineral oils are not so good.

In a pinch gay men have been known to use anything that is at hand, such as hair oil, margarine, mayonnaise, lard, and salad oil. Once a friend used some green goddess dressing. We asked him how it worked, and he said fine except the smell made him and his partner hungry.

However inventive you get, do not use greases from the tool shed. Automobile lubes and 3-in-One oil have their uses, but sex is not one of them.

Attitudes toward sex

A great many gay men feel that sexual pleasure is where one finds it, but not everyone you meet will have that opinion. For some, anal intercourse is fine if they're on top, but the passive role is considered effeminate. Others may feel that getting sucked off is fine but that doing the sucking is terrible.

As a rule, these and similar ideas stem from hangups about homosexuality. Whatever act a man scorns to do, that is the act that, by his own set of rules, would define him as gay. Thus he rules himself straight, no matter how attracted to his own sex he may be. Others may make good-bad differentiations among the common sex practices so they can commit the "bad" ones, and then enjoy a punishing sense of guilt afterwards.

If you prefer one kind of sex to another, that's fine and normal; we all have our tastes. But if you let your fears dictate your activities, you're cramping your style and losing out on pleasure.

Men who have functioned for a time in the straight world should note two things: first, most gay men are not into male-female roles in sex. This exists, but as a variant and not the rule. Second, both partners should have the opportunity to ejaculate. For one reason or another a guy may not want to get off, have reciprocation, or reverse positions. However, the cavalier attitude some hetero men display toward females does not go down well in the gay world.

Finally, remember that a man's body type, his way of dressing, his manner in the bars, or his cock size do not necessarily define his preferences in bed. Mr. Muscles may prefer to be passive, Don Donkeydick may be bored silly with having to do the fucking all the time, and Little Cutey may be a masterful stud. Do not, as the old saying goes, judge a book by its cover.

Having some class

A man makes a date with you, then fails to show up and does not give you the courtesy of a phone call. A guy says you can stay all night, then hustles you out the door the moment sex is over. In a bar someone spends a good deal of time leading you on, then exits alone (having gotten his jollies in the tease). A man assures you that he lives alone or with "just a roommate," but while you two are having sex his lover comes in, and you find yourself in the middle of an ugly scene. These are a few examples of the bad manners indulged in by an appreciable minority of gay men. Most of us are not to be faulted, but we are not that great a majority. Several factors make it all too easy for gay men to conduct themselves badly with one another.

With an active sex life that involves a number of different partners, it's not hard to begin thinking of other gay men as mere sexual appliances rather than as people. Some homosexuals feel that since society rejects them, they will reject society including its courtesies. Self-hatred lies behind both these attitudes. This becomes clear when you notice that almost inevitably the foul-mannered gay man limits his lack of consideration to other gays. By the logic of self-hatred, there is no reason to extend to a fag the thoughtfulness that is automatic in dealings with heterosexuals.

None of us is perfect, everyone has a bad day now and again, and being gay may give us reasons. But it does not provide excuses. Nobody is let off from acting decently. If you find you are developing a double standard of manners, one way with gays, another way with straights, or casual with sex partners, formal otherwise, then take this as a danger signal. And don't put up with rudeness from other gay men; call them on it.

Dr. Alex Comfort writes in his *Sex in Society* that it "seems reasonable to regard sexual intercourse as an important recreation which is biologically very well adapted to release residual anxieties of all kinds. . . . It is, in other words, the healthiest and most important human sport. . . ." All we can add is that sports and games are always more fun when you learn to play them well.

8 First Love

When I see him lying naked, I feel like saying mass on his chest.

— Jean Genet

You've met this guy and he's just wonderful! Great, there's nothing like love. And there's little so dreary as having to give the following advice, but like anything else passions can make problems.

First, it's very easy to confuse the ecstasy of love with the elation that comes from sexual discovery and exploration. This is especially so if you are very young, if you have previously restrained your impulses or had semi-faked or otherwise unsatisfactory sex with women.

Second, some men unconsciously feel that love justifies their sexual orientation but that mere horniness does not, so they may excessively elevate relationships in order not to feel guilty.

Third, younger men especially may want to believe they love somebody mainly because they are finding it tough to be independent and go it alone.

Fourth, if a guy is all starry-eyed, a man of greater experience can easily take advantage of him. Even if he does not push buttons, even if it is the real thing, value systems including definitions of love may differ widely. Two humans rarely love equally, and love, alas, does not always last forever.

In short, the delightful state of being in love should

qualify the lover for an insurance policy, but it doesn't. You have to take care of yourself. Therefore, no matter how sure you are that This Is It and he is Mr. Right, *keep your money separate.* Don't sign papers, for instance, that make you second party to a mortgage or guarantor for a loan. Don't lend or invest money, don't open a joint checking account. (What you *should* do is discussed in Chapter 16.)

This may sound cynical and cold, but if it's real love, there'll be plenty of time to build mutual trust. And if it's a passing fancy, or if a charming rat has led you down the garden path, you can experience a broken heart without the distraction of financial ruin.

Age does not give immunity from the follies of love. Plenty of older men have been taken to the cleaners by young guys who turned out to be less appealing than they first seemed. If you are an older man whose relationship with a younger man has a financial side to it, be sure it does not get out of hand. Be especially alert when the pressure is on for more, more, more. Remember that you have leverage, too: he is not the only negotiable young man in the world.

Another problem is falling in love with a straight man. This is a no-win situation, and most experienced homosexual men will go out of their way to avoid it. Sure, your hetero friend may be pleasant, even understanding, but that doesn't mean he will go for anything physical. If he should, it's not likely to be real loving but rather a situation where you would do all the work and he would get all the fun.

True, there are gay men who seduce straight men, but in most cases this is more of a challenging hobby than a matter of love. Experience, cleverness, and a good sense of human psychology are indispensable. And those few gay men who are hung up on straight guys must make themselves available for what they can get, which physically is very little and emotionally is nothing at all.

If you should find that your affections always seem to flow toward straight or otherwise unsuitable men, ask yourself if maybe you are making a self-punishment out of frustration. Are you trying to avoid dealing with your sexuality by substituting difficulties for relationships?

Leaving the sorrows and traps aside, let's assume that your beloved *is* wonderful and that you two want to have an intimate, long-term relationship. The first thing to realize is that the standard heterosexual role models are not very useful for gay men. And second, male sexuality is often specific and urgent and is excited by the idea of a variety of partners. "Promiscuity" is the loaded epithet.

The big question, then, is this: how are two men to relate to each other so the result is worth the trouble?

They must create their own scene, tailoring it to their individual needs and abilities. In our experiences the most successful alliances are those where the Mom-&-Pop role is most thoroughly ignored. The lover who is on top in bed may be the one who cooks and cleans. His beloved may lead on the dance floor, decorate the apartment, and keep the car in repair. Each one acts as nurse when the other is ill.

Sexually speaking, perfect fidelity is a lovely idea, but it is not terribly common in straight marriages, and among gay couples it is not always highly valued, even as an ideal. For one thing, casual sex is often easily available to gay men, which helps greatly to emphasize the fact that fucking can be one thing and love another. Second, gay men are men, both on the same side of the double standard that makes it all right for straight males to fool around but wrong for their wives to do so.

Some gay male couples will have a monogamous relationship. Some will mess around only when one of the two goes off on a trip. Others may go out cruising together or arrange three-ways. Many different arrangements can be made, and in our view the important thing for gay men who are lovers is not necessarily sexual fidelity as such, but that they adopt a suitable set of rules in the matter of sex and then follow them with great care. This is the sort of faithfulness most likely to pay off.

Obviously, if every relationship must be formed individually instead of blindly following hetero stereotypes, and if gay male lovers have to be both husband and wife to each other, then frankness is important.

Lovers must sit down together every so often and clear

the air. Sometimes it's painful, but even the closest of couples can have misunderstandings. And all relationships require adjustments now and again, especially relationships that are custom-made, not ready-to-wear. Without a basic frankness supporting the relationship it is likely to evaporate, leaving nothing but its obligations, and these will soon begin to look like huge, unprofitable burdens. And another potentially good pairing goes down the drain.

Finding a lover

The perfect love-object is a universal fantasy among all humans and is commonly idealized in works of art. Your own version of Mr. Perfect, delightful as it may be, can easily get in the way of real-life relationships. You can suspect the worst if you keep rejecting possible lovers with "Yes, but...." But what? Do you really expect to find Superman flying into your life? And isn't he already involved with Lois Lane (and, who knows, possibly also with Jimmy Olson)? And remember, too, that you yourself are not any kind of ideal being, but a man. Whoever your lover may be, you two will have to tolerate a certain number of imperfections in each other.

Worse yet is to believe that once you find your ideal lover, he will wave his magic wand and fix all that is wrong with your life. Obviously that's impossible, but it's easy to drift into thinking this, especially for younger men.

This doesn't mean you should settle for any male who is unattached and breathing. Just don't allow your impossible dream to raise your expectations beyond all real hope of fulfillment.

Remember, too, that if you want a lover you must be available. Most couples will tell you that they happened to meet only by the most miraculous of chances. If you stay home and merely wish that Mr. Right would appear, you're reducing the possibility of meeting him to zero.

Not finding a lover

Many gay men choose not to become deeply involved with another, preferring casual relationships. This mode of life has the advantages of mobility, variety, and freedom; it also has its drawbacks. Sheer nerve-ending sex, rarely or never including deep affection, can eventually become boring. Then you're likely to seek out a variety of stimuli, and sooner or later you can end up jaded. A lack of involvement with other people can eventually create a pervasive feeling of emptiness in some men, a sense that the world is a dreary, worthless place. The danger here is that this morbid outlook may be countered by excessive residence in those artificial paradises created by alcohol and drugs.

As a gay man you have to make your own way in the area of intimate relationships, since the world provides you with few useful examples to follow. However, with more and more homosexuals coming out of the closet and trying to live as suits them best, a great deal of trial-and-error experimentation is going on. Today's generation of gay men may contribute a variety of tested man-to-man relationships as a legacy to the future.

9 The Older Gay Man

> ...many faces within its face — the face of the child, the boy, the young man, the not-so-young man — all present still....
>
> — Christopher Isherwood

The older man coming out, say from age thirty on up, faces some problems — physical, psychological, social, and legal — that differ from those of the younger man.

Physical considerations

While the youth fixation of American culture has frequently been noted, it is nothing compared to that in the more visible areas of the gay world. Everyone, it seems, is under twenty-five and beautiful with nary a wrinkle, an ounce of fat, or a grey hair. The older a man is, the more discouraging he will find the scene; by and large, the gorgeous kids aren't going to be much interested in him.

Fortunately, there is more to gay life than cruise bars and discos, and there's plenty of room for the older man. However, at any age a good deal of emphasis is put on appearance, so the older man who is coming out should take careful stock of himself and consider what improvements he can make.

This step is especially important for men who have been leading an ostensibly straight existence, where physical neglect and sartorical sloppiness are, to gay eyes, excessively tolerated. Consciously or not, some men troubled about their sex role will dress badly so they'll be unattractive to both women and men.

Many older men are overweight, and find themselves too busy to take up the sort of rigorous exercise and dieting that would enable them to drop those last few pounds. Even so, a gay man can expect to make out better if he's only ten pounds overweight, not fifty.

If you are clearly too heavy, try to get off as much of the excess poundage as you can. You may simply be eating too much all along the line, or maybe you've developed a snacking habit, or you crave large amounts of beer and can't leave the French bread alone. Sit down and figure out what's making you overweight. In any case, avoid crash or fad diets. Gradual loss is the best way to get the weight off and keep it off.

One hidden source of calories is drinking. A twelve-ounce bottle of beer provides 160 to 180 calories; more for ales. Soda pop and other sweet mixers run 12 to 15 calories per ounce, and the average drink contains about two ounces. Add an ounce and a half of gin and you may have 200 calories in the glass. Help yourself to a handful of salted nuts, and that's another 60 to 80 calories.

The least fattening drink is hard liquor, taken straight and slow, or mixed with water (no calories) or club soda (less than one calorie per ounce).

Exercise will tone up your body, make the skin look better, and improve your health. How much you work out depends on your inclination and circumstances, but remember this basic rule: the exercise program that you *will* do, however modest, is infinitely superior to the one you won't bother with, however ambitious.

The older you are, the wiser it is to get checked out by your doctor before embarking on a diet or exercise program. And of course if you have a medical problem, diet or exercise plans should be undertaken only with your physician's supervision.

Now consider your hair. Does the cut really suit your face? Have you been settling for years for the standard Joe-&-Louie's Barbershop job? Have you fewer hairs than you'd like to have, and perhaps an excessive amount of ear? A good hair stylist can do wonders. It will cost more than Joe-&-Louie's, but the results can be well worth it.

Over the years you may have established bad habits of posture, a "student slouch" of the shoulders, say, or letting your stomach stick out. You might have to correct any big problems within the frame of your exercise program, but most of them will be slight and can be cleared up with little trouble. One friend of ours looked a huge blob when seated in his usual overly-relaxed manner on a bar stool. When he sat up, though, out came a great pair of shoulders and a nice big chest. These easily put into proportion the few extra pounds he had around his waist. Once our friend realized this, he began to persist in sitting up. He began making out more and better and hasn't slumped since.

Some older men look to plastic surgery to take off the years. It can be useful, but don't expect miracles. Good work is expensive. Cheap work may look awful. Two operations are not uncommon among gay men: the blepharoplasty or eye-job, to reduce pouches, and the face-tightener nicknamed the tuck-and-roll.

In great part, facial aging comes about because the head muscles are very little used; many people are unaware that any muscles exist beyond the borders of the face itself. Sagging can be retarded and matters can sometimes even be improved a bit, if the load hasn't shifted too much, by the regular use of isometric exercises. This is the poor man's plastic surgery. It can be quite effective and leaves no scars. (The bibliography lists references to more detailed information on both surgery and isometrics.)

How are your teeth? They make a great difference in your appearance, adding or subtracting years in some cases. If you're going to be smiling and socializing, you must have your mouth in good shape and your breath sweet. Men who wear false teeth should be especially careful about keeping their choppers impeccable; denture breath, even a little, is not conducive to intimacy.

Give a thought to your clothes. They can emphasize what's best and camouflage the rest. Remember that extremely youthful styles are likely to make you look grotesque, not younger.

In bars or other public places, always show yourself in the best light, literally. People look their nicest in diffuse light with lots of yellow in it, which is why candle glow is considered so romantic. Stay away from harsh glares, whether from electric lamps or daylight pouring in through a window, and avoid the discoloring rays of fluorescent illumination.

Carelessly lighting a cigarette can add years to your lines and lines to your years. Hold the match at a distance as it flares up, bringing it to the cigarette only when it calms to a minimal flame. Keep lighters set at the lowest level of function. These light sources are single and very concentrated, perfect to exaggerate the merest line, wrinkle, or sag.

Whatever physical improvements you choose to make, the general idea is not to reverse the clock but to look your best. Making the most of what you have is one thing, striving for eternal youth is something else altogether. (Some gay men do attempt it, with efforts that reach the heroic; they may succeed in kidnapping time for a while, but eventually they begin to look somewhat strange, as if a mixture of true youth and wax-museum immortality.)

Some signs of passing years can add to your looks rather than detract from them. Many a face that is basically blah in youth will improve with the appearance of a few little accent lines here and there.

Magazine advertisements, cosmetics counters, and corset shops all offer a variety of coverups for the various evidences of aging. As a rule, though, the more artifice employed, the more artificial the result. In this time the natural look is very much the fashion, and the day of the bewigged, touched-up, cinched-in exquisite is long over.

If you must use something to improve on nature, get the very best product you can afford. While a balding head can be sexy and have pleasing contours, a bad hairpiece is worse than nothing.

Psychological problems

The difficulties facing the older man are likely to have two sources. First, he may get tangled up in assumptions derived from his straight style of existence in the past. Second, the passage into the gay world may induce a reaction unique to the man who is no longer young.

Maybe you've been gay as a goose all along, but if you played it straight for any amount of time, then you probably picked up a lot of notions that are not valid for gay men. In the last chapter we pointed out that hetero sex roles do not usually apply to gay love relationships. Especially if you are coming out from a marriage which was satisfying except for the sex, then the temptation will be great to re-create the situation with a male partner. This can lead to a lot of difficulties and disappointments.

Many men have quite an adjustment to make once they turn from relations with females to those of their own sex. For women, face and body are not the only attractions; on occasion they may have very little importance. Charm, breeding, cuteness, sexiness, any number of things can exert a compelling influence, even including ugliness, weakness, or physical disability. Males are more likely to be turned on only by physical attributes, at least to start with. Thus, many a newly-out older gay man comes to realize that he is viewed by other gay males the way he has viewed women — as a sex object. This is a shock that he will have to get over as quickly as he can.

Whether a man has been involved with women or not, if he comes out as gay when he is on the far side of thirty, one special cross is his to bear: there is very often an overwhelming temptation to make up for the years of suppressed desires and rejected opportunities. He then takes off in frantic pursuit of sexual encounters. After a while, typically, he sees that his adventures in the present only highlight the sexual bleakness in his past and can't erase it. Once this becomes clear, a state of melancholy may set in.

The important thing in handling this syndrome is to recognize it as the inevitable, poignant reaction it is. Usually it passes soon enough; the sufferer becomes more fully integrated into his new lifestyle and begins to add gay experiences to his memory.

Social problems

There are two main areas of difficulty here, that of relating with a much younger man and that of locating gay men of one's own age.

Strong as the emphasis on youth can be in the gay world, an appreciable number of young men do in fact actively seek relationships with older males. Their reasons vary, so the mature man can find himself presented with a fine opportunity in some cases or faced with big trouble in others.

Proportionally speaking, successful May-December relationships seem to be much more common among gays than straights. A paternal sort of lover can be very attractive to the many young gay men who have not enjoyed closeness with parents, particularly with their fathers. Also, the older man is likely to be settled into a career, with a permanent place to live, and a healthy bank account; thus he has achieved the certainty and steadiness in life that a young man, still adrift in the world, can find very comforting to associate with.

Of course the great danger in older-younger scenes is that the more youthful partner may be a gold digger. The term sounds old-fashioned, but the type has hardly died out. If you are a mature man you must exercise elementary caution when getting involved with anyone who is a good deal younger. And you must realize that you are putting yourself in the same position as the older straight man does when he is attracted to much younger women. You cannot offer youth in exchange for youth; you must offer what benefits time and experience have brought you.

On the simplest level this may mean money. It gives access to life's pleasures — entertainment, sports events, travel, fine food and drink — which can be enjoyed in the company of an appreciative younger man.

As an older man you can offer sympathy, know-how, kindness, understanding. Remember that especially in big cities a young gay man can lead a busy life, having many acquaintances and lots of sex, and still feel very much alone. He may greatly admire someone who will actually listen to him.

Your hobby, your social life, your job, these or any such

interesting facets of your existence might help attract the notice of younger men. A photographer friend finds it helpful to let one or another young acquaintance hang around his studio while he's working.

And there is always a young man's vanity. This does not mean you tell him he's handsome. If he is, he knows it, and in this case, if you want him to focus on you, comment on how well he manages whatever tiny physical defect he may have. This technique has to be used with care, so you don't appear nasty or rejecting, but it has a rather odd effect on the prettier people: they think you are seeing *them*, not just projecting your desires on their looks. This may be worth more to them than yards of compliments.

Whatever the younger man's looks, you may interest him by turning yourself into a mirror. That is, you listen, you appear wise and sympathetic, you say back to the young man what he says to you, in slightly different phrasing, of course, and he may end up so enchanted with self-love as to find you irresistible.

All these means of attracting younger men require time. A party is better for this sort of thing than the bars, and a quiet dinner is better yet.

Assuming that a relationship is established, certain problems may come up that are inherent in the age difference itself. For instance, if you really can't stand the popular music currently in favor with the young and your lover feels deprived when he's not wallowing in it, then there's going to be friction. Or, you may have to explain half the things you want to talk about, and you can find it as boring to be the teacher as your young lover can find it tedious to be lectured. Or your sexual needs may vary greatly from your lover's. A friend of ours confided that he didn't know whether he could hold out until the day when his younger lover would decide that he too wanted sex only every other night.

Finally, it is almost impossible to avoid the role of father in the relationship; after all, the young man who likes older guys most likely wants to play son. This may be unconscious, but it's almost certain to be an important element. Problems then arise if the older man does not feel fatherly;

he himself might like to be taken care of, or prefer a more egalitarian relationship. On the other hand, if he plays Daddy, even the younger man who likes this and desires a certain amount of supervision may still at times resent it and react with rebellion.

In these roles there is a danger for the younger man and a temptation for the older one. Where the elder assumes the primary responsibility for decision-making and for finances, the younger man may never achieve personal maturity, the ability to stand on his own two feet and make his own money. The older man may prefer the younger one dependent, but this is often destructive to the latter, who in a long-term relationship might some day have to assume responsibilities his aged partner can no longer handle.

In summary, if you are an older man for whom young men are the only way to go, keep these things in mind:

1. Since you can't compete well with youth on youth's ground, get younger men to play your game with your deck. And hold on to the deal, always.

2. You must give something in return for something. It needn't be money; sympathy, skill, status, charm, any number of things can be offered.

3. Expect to take some time to interest a young man. Only physical attraction is instantaneous; everything else works gradually.

4. Don't let go of your dignity. Avoid appearing weak or troubled. Don't talk about your problems.

5. Remember that youth is not a rare quantity in the world. If one young man doesn't work out, there are plenty more.

6. Speak up. If matters don't seem to be developing naturally, a nice mix of frankness and friendliness can get a good scene going or bring a pointless one to an end. You may only have to say something like, "My interest in you is more than just social; I wonder how you feel about me."

7. Don't come on hard, demanding your money's (and time's) worth. You may not want to think of yourself as a sucker, but remember that the younger man does not care to think that he is being bought and

paid-for. A feeling of gratefulness and pleasure in your company are far more likely to bring him to your bed than any sense of obligation.

8. Except possibly in very Grand Amour situations, don't expect perfect sexual fidelity from a younger man. Settle for the virtue of discretion.

9. In a relationship, work to make the adjustments mutual, as far as feasible. If all is arranged to suit only one party (a young man with many demands and whims, say, or an older man who will not change his set ways), then the coupling is sure to be brief.

The second social difficulty, locating middle-aged and older gay men, arises from the fact that as a group these gays are far more closeted than their younger brethren. When these men were young there was no gay liberation movement, and the legal protection of the rights of anyone identified as homosexual was likely to be spotty, at best. Long accustomed to a sexually invisible existence, they rarely want to make any drastic changes in their lifestyle at this point in life.

Partly as a result, many older gay men devote much of their time to professional and recreational associations of the straight world. And their gay social life may largely or exclusively center about private entertaining in homes.

Thus the usual gay social institutions prove useful only to a limited extent. In most cities certain bars will have a majority of older men as customers. Sometimes this fact is mentioned in guidebooks; otherwise you'll have to shop around or go by word of mouth. It's a rare bar owner who will advertise his place as catering to a mature crowd; he doesn't want it to be considered a "wrinkle room."

While some of these places may be fun and lively, often they are depressing, full of alcoholics or hustlers or both. And a good many older gay men don't frequent the bars at all.

The baths are similar to the bars; in large population centers a few steam baths may cater to the older crowd. Some or all of the others may discourage or bar mature men from entering.

Some older men report considerable success in using classified ads in gay publications. Some rap groups have arrangements for older men to meet on certain nights, and in larger cities there are introduction services.

If this all sounds discouraging, you *can* find good company with men of similar age and interests, but you must invest a bit of work and patience. First get to know one or two or three older men, then through them meet their friends.

If you have a casual acquaintance you think may be gay, try dropping a few hairpins. Don't worry about whether he interests you sexually. Social is what counts: he may have friends who will prove attractive to you when, via him, you meet them.

Legal problems

For the most part these are limited to the gay man who has children. You may jeopardize your visitation rights if you are living with a lover, and if you have custody of your offspring, the courts may not permit you to keep the children if you bring a lover into your household.

Because your ex-wife and your children may have actual or potential claims upon your finances, it is even more vital for you than for other gay men to make legal arrangements, including a will, that cover all the important aspects of your life.

On the positive side

It's a common notion among heterosexuals (unwittingly echoed by some gays) that older homosexuals invariably lead an unhappy, lonely existence. The facts, however, would appear to be otherwise. Sociologists Weinberg and Williams summarized a study in which " . . . older respondents report more positive self-images, fewer perceived shortcomings, fewer problems and feelings of self-doubt, and more satisfaction in their jobs and interpersonal relationships." They conclude that, by the measure of various psychological dimensions, older homosexual men are not worse off than younger ones and in some ways are actually better off.

At twenty-five, a man is likely to find it difficult to relate to anyone who is ten or even five years his senior or junior. This lessens with time until, at forty-five, say, a decade of age difference between two men is insignificant. Thus an older man's range of acquaintance can be interestingly wide and varied, and his chances of meeting a suitable life-partner are all the greater.

The older man is done with the painful process of growing up and probably has established himself financially. Sexually, there are no more doubts about whether to try to outgrow a homosexual phase or to suppress one's gay side by a frantic plunge into the heterosexual mainstream. In short, if the benefits of youth are gone, so are its difficulties and distractions.

10 The Underage Gay

Growth is the only evidence of life.
— Cardinal Newman

As a result of the social turmoil in the United States during the 1960s, the age of eighteen became generally established as the point at which a person is legally an adult. Anyone younger, by law, is a minor or underage.

Large segments of society find it impossible to accept the idea that even adults can be permitted to be homosexual, and this view becomes almost universal in terms of people who are underage. For that matter, most adults in the United States do not look kindly upon the idea of their minor children engaging in even heterosexual sex, so the gay variety is absolutely unthinkable. This view is strongly reflected in the laws and institutions of American society.

Underage and the law

The legal regulations relating to underaged persons are a crazyquilt of variations from state to state, so it is not possible here to discuss them specifically. In general, though, the laws are intended to protect minors from two things, their own immaturity and inexperience, and exploitation by adults. Usually, the younger the underage person the greater the extent of society's protection.

Typically, if you are below a specified age, you are

presumed to be incapable of consenting to any sort of sexual activity; you're considered to be the victim of your older partner, even if the sex was your idea and you thoroughly enjoyed it. If you are caught the usual thing is for you to be sent home to your parents for closer supervision. However, if you are found to be beyond their control, or if they disown you, you can be declared a ward of the court. Then you will probably be placed in a foster home or an institution.

Once you reach the age of consent you may still legally be a minor, and if you're caught engaging in gay sex, that's an act for which you can be charged in juvenile court. Usually you have few of the protections enjoyed by adult defendants: no right to bail, no jury trial, and requirements for proof of the offense may be less rigorous. The judge can make a wide range of rulings if he finds you guilty, from sending you home on probation to shipping you off to the state reformatory.

Although ordinary gay sex acts are now legal between consenting adults in many places, they are often still crimes if one or both partners are underage.

In summary, any underage gay who is having a sex life should keep it as secret as possible.

Meeting other gays
Some large cities have coffee houses for gay teenagers. Many high schools have an invisible underground of gay students. Usually there is a "chicken coop" somewhere around, often a doughnut shop or hamburger stand, and as a rule it quickly becomes known, first to older men who like very young men, and then to the police.

Gay teenagers sometimes hang out in front of gay bars, hoping to meet customers as they're coming or going. This is not a good idea. The law can come down on minors with any number of charges, from loitering or violating curfew to soliciting or prostitution. Adult gay men, even if older by only a few years, are often afraid to get involved with anyone underage; they could be charged with child molestation, corruption of a minor, or sodomy, all of which are serious crimes.

Medical problems

Today, minors usually can be treated for venereal disease without parental knowledge or permission. If you are an underage gay man and believe you have some kind of sexually transmitted disease, telephone the nearest health department for information. You do not have to give your name, all you say will be kept confidential, and the number will not appear on your family's phone bill if you make your call from a phone booth.

If you are close to eighteen in years or appearance, when you are questioned at the VD clinic you can describe some casual pickup. If you are closer to fourteen, say, then you may get much closer questioning. Clinic staff members or a private doctor may fear that you're involved in hustling or are the victim of a child molester. A vague but heterosexual encounter with an older woman — she was driving through, picked you up hitchhiking, etc. — may serve as sufficient explanation.

Where no public health or VD clinic is available with its free services, you might try going to a private physician by yourself, especially if he is your family doctor and has known you for a long time. Be careful, though, if he has impressed you in the past as extremely moralistic or fanatically religious.

However sympathetic and understanding, the doctor expects to be paid. And you don't want his bill to go to the house. Bring enough money to cover the cost of the appointment, and pay him at the end of it. If you have to borrow the cash, try a sympathetic older male relative or close family friend. If you are sure your VD infection has come from a sex partner who is an adult, he may be willing to pay the bill.

Do not take whatever medications happen to be in the bathroom cabinet. They won't cure you of what you've got, and they may make you sick in some other way as well. And do not bother with any home remedies, patent medicines, or alleged cures that you hear about from school friends. They will not work.

The important thing is to get treatment at once. And you must be sure to inform anyone that you may have exposed to the disease. After treatment you should not have sex with others until you are certain that you are completely cured and cannot infect your partner.

Many gay people have described their adolescent years as full of hardship and unhappiness, usually because they felt different from the other kids. Where the difference was detectable, school often became a nightmare. And some, when their parents found out about them, were kicked out of the house and left to fend for themselves.

Your personal situation may be bad, but consider the alternatives. Running away to some big city merely puts you into competition with a lot of other underage men for the few jobs that may be available aside from the dead-end of hustling. You will live in constant fear of being picked up by the police. If you're sent to a foster home or to some sort of juvenile-authority institution, well, sexual abuse of persons known to be gay, or even suspected of it, is not uncommon.

Legally, you can leave home to go out on your own only if your parents agree to it. Even then, if the state is not satisfied with the arrangements made for your housing and supervision, it can step in and send you off to an institution. If your home situation becomes genuinely too intolerable to bear, it might be wisest to see if your parents will consent to your living elsewhere, with a sympathetic relative, at the home of a classmate, school counselor, or whomever.

It may be best to just keep cool. When you are sixteen the two years before you become of age may seem an eternity. They are not really that long a time, however, when you think of your entire life. Is it worth screwing that up by doing something rash, when all you have to do to get your freedom is simply wait for it to come to you?

Whatever choice you feel you must make, remember that you are going to want a job one of these days and that most of them require a certain amount of education. If you can't finish high school, remember that you can study in night school free or very cheaply, and you can take the G.E.D. test for the equivalent of a high school diploma.

Probably it is accurate to say that the underage homosexual suffers the most from the discrimination against gay people. Unfair, you say? Yes, it is. But that's the way it is. The gay world will be a lot more pleasant and the straight scene a lot easier to deal with after you turn eighteen.

11 The Gay Minorities

I. S & M

When we think that we are experimenting on others, we are really experimenting on ourselves.

— Oscar Wilde

Sadist and masochist, slave and master, active and passive, topman and bottom — whatever you call it, S&M has a small but definite place in the gay world, just as it has among heterosexuals.

The varied practices of S&M add up to fantasies of dominance and submission; pain and physical restraint often play a prominent part in the action. S&M sex is not, as many people assume, the same thing as physical assault. It's a voluntary, cooperative means of reaching sexual satisfaction. S&M is not a form of mayhem, it's a kind of drama.

Most newcomers to the gay world are not interested in S&M, but a few do prefer it from the start. Others may want to investigate it out of curiosity, and some men like the S&M bar scene for its masculine ambience if nothing else. Whatever your interest in this part of the gay world, this is briefly how it functions.

Finding the S&M bar. Check gay guides and local gay publications, then go and investigate. In recent years many gay bars and gay men have taken up the he-man image and fetishy styles of dress, so it's easy to find places with the appearance of S&M but little or none of its reality. In the true S&M bar the customers appear about as rugged as their clothing, and the age range is thirty years and up.

Who is there. Though the range of dress is narrow — biker, construction worker, street tough, cowboy — the variety of interests is wide. Some men are costume trippers, others are fetishists, still others have interests that may or may not be strictly S&M, such as fisting, enemas, or urine trips. As already mentioned, these bars also attract men who merely like a macho atmosphere. And there are men who are sadistically inclined (liking to give pain, to dominate), their counterparts the masochists, and a good many who enjoy both S and M.

Making out. Image is all-important. In your daily life you may be some glittering combination of youth, wit, charm, beauty, and wealth, but what counts in the S&M world is masculinity. You must dress butch, walk butch, talk butch. And leave the cologne in the bottle.

Classically the M, subtly encouraged by the S, makes the approach. Often enough, however, the two merely begin conversation as in any gay bar. After openers, the talk will differ markedly from the usual bar conversation. Sexual interests will be discussed very freely. To a newcomer this may seem like no more than an indulgence in cheap thrills, but it is necessary to match up desires. The whips-and-chains gent and the guy who likes enemas are not likely to find each other very interesting in bed.

Whatever the content of the conversation, remember that judgment on another's sex scene, however ridiculous it may strike you, is strictly taboo, as is any expression of irony or amusement. We all tend to be extremely self-indulgent in constructing our fantasies, and we all know some of them would seem extremely silly if we revealed them to others. In this kind of bar private fantasies become public, which means that a certain amount of tolerance is required all around. That very tough biker, sinister in black leather, standing so macho at the bar, one gleaming black boot planted firmly on the brass foot-rail, may be a clerk at Macy's.

You may have heard about a dress code that signals who wants what. There is one, but it's not very dependable. Many men indicate that they are S's, even some who don't actually care for S&M as such, because they like the rough-tough image it suggests. Others, though they are M's by nature, prefer to negotiate sex scenes from the S side of the street. Some men signal one way but will go the other if they meet a suitable partner. And many guys don't bother with the code at all.

For what it's worth, these are the signs and signals of the dress code.

Items worn on the left side of the body indicate that the man is S/dominant/active/top; on the right they mark the M/submissive/passive/bottom. Keys and handkerchiefs are the principal indicators. The former are hung from belt loops at the hip, left or right, and occasionally, when a man goes both ways, down the middle of his backside.

The cambric cowboy-style hankies are more informative: dark blue to signal an interest in anal sex, red for fisting. Less often you may spot handkerchiefs that are black (whipping), brown (feces), yellow (urine), or orange (anything). There are other meanings for other colors, but their use is even less in evidence, and this elaboration has suspiciously commercial overtones.

Thus, a man with a dark blue hanky in the left back pocket of his jeans supposedly wants to fuck.

Jacket chains, looped through the left or right epaulet, indicate whether the wearer considers himself active or passive.

As a newcomer, your lack of experience will be something of a drawback. Do not say you do everything and anything, just to see what will happen. You may find yourself deep into some scene that you haven't bargained for. Be vague about your own likes and dislikes, and if something proposed to you sounds agreeable, make it clear that you haven't had much experience but are eager to find out more.

For those who are serious about S&M it is customary to

serve an apprenticeship as an M to an experienced S. This holds even for men who feel they themselves are strictly the S type. "You can't understand the one without experiencing the other," is standard wisdom here. Certainly there is a good deal to learn because this sort of sex can cover a lot of territory, calls for the use of potentially dangerous equipment and activity, and requires a heightened awareness of self and partner in interaction.

S&M action. As must be clear by now, there is no one single pattern of S&M sex. It can be mostly verbal, it can involve the use of restraints, devices for punishment, means of humiliation, and usually there's a marked amount of clothes fetishism.

Sex may occur in bed, but men who take S&M seriously will have a blackroom. Usually this is a windowless, soundproofed chamber painted some dark color.

Because the man new to this mode of eroticism may be confused, he and his partner should agree beforehand on some certain word or gesture as a distress signal. Many experienced S&M partners always make this arrangement, at least until they know each other well enough to do without it.

Dangers. Ominous as the world of sadomasochism may seem to the outsider and the newcomer, there are only four things to bear in mind at all times. First, the S&M scene does have an occasional psychotic personality, able to disguise his sociopathic desires as mere sadomasochistic fun-and-games. Protect yourself by knowing your sex partners; go with the guys you see around the bar a lot. If you meet somebody via the mail, arrange to meet him at a bar or somewhere so you can check his vibes before you get together in private. Always avoid anybody who is drunk or doped-up.

Second, watch out with the various kinds of equipment. For your heart's sake it is best never to mess with any electric shock device. Be sure there is a handle on anything put into the rectum. Pushed far enough inside, a vibrator or whatever can become stuck in the turns of the sticky-walled colon and will have to be removed by a doctor. Third, take great care if you mix drugs and any kind of heavy-duty sex. Except among a few classical practitioners of S&M, the use of booze and pills and powders is a common way to heighten the experience. It's easy to get carried away, with each partner urging the other farther on until one loses control. Transcendent and painless as it may seem at the time, remember that you have to use your body the next day and for the rest of your life. And if one man passes out while the other is in restraints, the latter could find himself in a life-threatening situation.

Finally, fisting can cause a great deal of harm. This increasingly popular act is often related to S&M activity because it partakes strongly of symbolic humiliation and physical assault. Fistfucking can cause infection if the rectum's mucous membrane is scratched or torn. And a puncture in the colon wall may easily lead to peritonitis and then death.

If you try fisting, be sure you and your partner know what you're doing. If you become feverish or otherwise show signs of illness afterwards, seek medical attention at once.

Other S&M scenes. In large cities one or two baths and private clubs may cater to the sadomasochistic crowd. Some of these places are quite down and dirty while others are very elaborate, having specialized rooms fitted out with shackles and slings and such, and which have to be reserved in advance.

Classified ads (as explained in Chapter 6) will guide you to the more specialized mailing clubs. A few magazines cater to the male gay S&M reader, and they of course have many pages of classifieds. These publications are available at adult book stores and sometimes in S&M bars.

S or M? If you are fascinated by this subculture, consider carefully the role you assume in it. Many men like to go both ways, but M's seem to outnumber S's by three or four to one. While the S may seem the more glamorous of the

two types, remember that S&M is a complementary relationship and that the first-rate M is as much sought-after as
is the expert S. For your own satisfaction, it's best to come
on as you feel.

Sadomasochistic practices can be used on occasion as a
spice for the plainer kinds of gay lovemaking, they can be
indulged in every so often according to mood, or S&M can
be a whole way of life. Those who don't care for the scene
see it as an exaggeration of supermacho masculinity,
stifling in its conformity of dress and manner, essentially a
species of transvestism. S&M's adherents find it extremely
fulfilling sexually, and they enjoy the high level of in-group
loyalty and friendship within the scene. A small but significant number of men see sadomasochism as the only way to
live.

II. TRANSVESTISM

And after all what is a lie? 'Tis but the truth in masquerade.
— Lord Byron

Commonly referred to as drag, transvestism is the practice
of wearing the clothes of the opposite sex. Cross-dressing is
universal; it dates from the earliest recorded history and
was often a part of religious ceremonies. In one way or
another it has always been an element in the theater, and
not only for comic relief: the roles of Electra and Ophelia, to
name two, were first played by men. Today transvestism
is most visible in that form of entertainment called the drag
show.

   Theories about the practice of cross-dressing are many: a
deifying of the opposite sex; a means of getting at its
supposed magical powers; a flight from reality or masculinity or responsibility. As for its cause, again there is a
wide choice. Take your pick among birth trauma, childhood relations with parents, genetics, or hormone
imbalance. As with so much in the area of sex, nobody can
say anything for sure.

   Many people hold mistaken notions about drag. It is by

no means exclusively a gay male practice. The great majority of transvestites (TVs) in the United States are heterosexual men, most of them married and fathers. For most gay men cross-dressing holds little or no interest. There are two degrees of transvestism. The first is drag for the fun of it, seen at costume parties or the Mardi Gras or on Halloween. The second level is far more serious, where the devoted transvestite spends much or all his time in female attire. Practically speaking, most true transvestites must lead double lives, spending the work day in overalls or a three-piece suit, then off to the ball in a lovely Halston.

Much as your devoted cross-dresser may enjoy Halloween, the transvestites' national holiday, all year long he is likely to lead a busy life of drag balls, charity affairs, coronations, and private social gatherings. Large or small, most cities and many towns have an empress, elected annually, and numerous other titled persons. In fact, because anti-gay feeling runs high among straight TVs ("Just because I like to get dolled-up doesn't mean I'm a goddam queer"), two separate drag scenes exist, one heterosexual and one homosexual.

There are similarities to the S&M world up to a point: outsiders are not welcomed readily; older, experienced drags often sponsor and teach younger ones; the majority of gay men look askance at this gowned subgroup; and within the scene there is a highly developed sense of loyalty.

Unlike the leather crowd, many drags do enjoy a little public attention now and then. This fondness for parading about, if indulged too publicly, can lead to encounters with toughs and problems with the law.

Psychologically speaking, transvestism can be a rough way to go. Few enough parents can accept a son as homosexual; fewer still can do so when he is wearing a dress. And drag often trips off a lot of hostility in other men. Gays can be worse on this score than straights. Heteros are far more threatened by a masculine homosexual than one they can view as freaky-amusing. Gay men, however, often loathe drags, blaming them for the negative stereotypes most people have of homosexuals.

Many drags manage a double life with skill. But others,

reacting to the sneers they get from gays and straights alike, have a poor opinion of themselves. Thus there is always the increased danger of constructing one's life as a form of self-punishment, complete with tangles with the police.

Where drag is. Drag bars are relatively rare. If there is none in your area, your best bet is to connect with the scene through whatever social activities are advertised in gay papers and on bar posters. There is a national organization which publishes a newsletter, and there are several mailing-clubs for transvestites.

Partly because of laws and ordinances and partly because of hostility from other customers, it is futile in most parts of the country to look for fellow TVs in ordinary gay bars.

Buying clothes. You can buy what you need "for my wife" in department stores, but of course you can't try on anything. Within the drag world you will find readier means of access to what you need, including dressmakers. And there is always mail-order. (If you worry about discovery, use postal money orders, not personal checks; order using your first initial instead of your full name; and rent a mailbox at the post office.)

Drag and the law. Traditionally it has been unlawful in this country for a man to impersonate a woman in public (except on Halloween), but some of these laws have been successfully challenged in recent years, and in many areas ordinances against cross-dressing are not enforced. Just be sure you know the local situation before you step out into the street in drag.

Genderfuck. If you see a bearded man in a gown cut so low that it shows his unshaved chest and hairy armpits, that's a genderfuck. This send-up of sex-role stereotyping is anathema to the usual run of drags, probably because it is neither entirely serious nor totally comic. This new wrinkle in the cross-dressing scene harks back to the ancient mythological divinity, the androgyne, who is both sexes at once, and it is more a way of making a statement playfully than a whole way of life.

Transvestism may not be an easy way of life for a man, though it is another normal variant, but like any existence it can be lived well or badly. If you feel that cross-dressing is your way, remember and take to heart the immortal phrase of the famous drag entertainer, Charles Pierce, who says, "It takes a *man* to wear a dress like this."

III. THE EFFEMINATE MAN

"There are many ways of being a man...."
— E. M. Forster

Unsure of himself, still boyish in mannerisms, many a very young man (gay or straight) will appear effeminate for a brief time in his life. In most cases this passes as he orients himself in the adult world. But some males remain definitely effeminate.

In some cultures, such men have been admired, appointed priests, and sought out as lovers. Here and now, though, fem guys find the world no easy place in which to live. Not all gays are fems, and not all fems are gay, but whatever they do in bed, out of it they are highly visible. Thus, being the only men that most people can identify, rightly or wrongly, as homosexual, their mannerisms largely form the stereotype of the gay man. This is accepted by most straights and even by many inexperienced gays.

Fems get a hard time from hetero males, often are shunned by other gays, and are the butt of sometimes cruel humor in the media. Needing the closet the most, they are the least capable of staying inside it. Even if he marries and fathers a large brood of children, the effeminate man is likely to be the subject of joking gossip.

In employment he is often subjected to a good deal of discrimination. He will be hired, if at all, only for low-status, low-pay positions involving little contact with other employees or with the public. In other areas where gays encounter discrimination — housing, for example — the effeminate homosexual gets the worst of it.

Finally, he has to deal with rejection by fellow gays, which is quite common. Observe how many personal ads in gay publications carry the phrase "No fems".

Faced with mockery and welcomes that are anything but warm, some fem homosexuals take to one or the other of two extremes. They will emphasize their mannerisms, camp it up outrageously all the time, and become screaming queens. Or, they will become razor-tongued with bitterness and probably give themselves up to self-hatred and self-destructiveness.

If you are effeminate, you do not have to make a road-show of necessity, though. There are other approaches to life besides the two above.

Some fems do well on the strength of their wit and personality. On the job such men are often accorded the status of court jester and can come to be regarded with considerable affection by their co-workers. One fem friend, for example, is adored by all the working housewives in the office because he shares his vast gourmet food knowledge with them in the form of delightfully conducted cooking courses.

To make the charming oddfellow situation work, the fem man has to closely follow two rules: he should never make fellow employees the targets of his wit (however tempting), and he should never make any mention of any kind of homosexual activities, even the innocent ones.

Another alternative is to live and work entirely within the gay world, perhaps among other fems. Though hassles will be fewer, they won't disappear, and good job opportunities are limited. It might be better to get training in some area of work that is heavily in demand, or to exploit some unique personal talent or skill. If you are the only guy in town who can appraise paintings or cane chairs, if you give the best poodle-clip for miles or have a genius for playing the stock market, how flitty you act won't matter a great deal.

There are two radical approaches. One is to be militant and stand up for your rights at all times. This is admirable, good for personal pride, and contributes to gay liberation. However, you have to learn and practice some form of self-defense. And unwavering militance can be immensely fatiguing and may lead to acute cynicism.

The other approach is to consciously rid yourself of effeminate mannerisms. However natural they feel, they are learned, not innate. They can be unlearned. To some fems the process of imitating masculine models of behavior would be more trouble than it's worth, and others will not allow themselves this remedy out of pride. But if you simply can't live with the difficulties of being effeminate, it is an option to consider.

If the fem gay man has a lot of ugly realities to face, that doesn't mean he has to accept the world on its worst behavior. One way or another, remember, existence is negotiable. The effeminate gay man who takes thought and plans well can be himself and enjoy his life.

IV. THE BOY-LOVER

Of course, there are no beings for whom love is perfectly easy, and it often exacts the encounter of beings who are set on different paths.

— Marcel Proust

The pederast or pedophile, the man who turns on to pre-teenage boys, will most often keep his desires a dark secret, not only from straights but from other gays as well. He is particularly loathed by most homosexual men because they not only disapprove of sex acts with children, but also feel the boy-lover, like the other minorities just discussed, is the cause of much of the strong prejudice against gays. When his activities are reported in the press, they reinforce the belief that all gay men lust for little boys as a matter of course.

In actuality, according to Weinberg in *Society and the Healthy Homosexual*, "child molestation is preponderantly a heterosexual practice," and he points out that the majority of men accused of molesting boys go on to marry women and raise families.

The pederast has much to fear from exposure besides social ostracism. Blackmailers adore boy-lovers and have been known to set them up in situations that are both compromising and photographable. Entanglements with the law mean registration as a sex pervert at the very least, possibly a criminal record, time spent in a mental institution, or, worse yet, a stretch in prison. Worse because the other inmates despise "child molesters," and the pederast will be lucky to get out alive.

Defenders of pedophilia argue that affection is harmless and should be expressed freely and physically, and that prohibitions against adult-child sex are nothing more than mere puritanism. But it is more complicated than that. There are certainly cases where boys benefit considerably from a relationship with an older man. Just as certainly, there are men who, even without using physical coercion, take advantage of their greater experience to pressure a boy into a relationship that he doesn't really want. Any man who is attracted to boys should try hard to understand this potential for manipulation, and to be sure he is not guilty of it.

The pedophile faces a life that is likely to be both difficult and dangerous, for there is little prospect that the laws and taboos banning such relationships will be relaxed in the forseeable future. Boy-lovers may find some support by joining the NAMBLA (North American Man/Boy Love Association; see bibliography).

As this chapter makes clear, human nature expresses itself in many and varied ways. Some of these styles of gay life may be distasteful to you. You may find it impossible to accept people whose existences differ remarkably from yours, or to understand the fulfillment they get from living as they do. But even so, as a cold, hard matter of tactics, we all benefit from strong mutual support. Like it or not, we are all a minority. We're all in this together.

12 Employment

America I'm putting my queer shoulder to the wheel.
— Allen Ginsberg

Typically almost half of a man's waking life is spent on the job. So it would be convenient, if nothing else, to be able to relax and be open about your sexual orientation at work. Gay activists point out that if all homosexuals identified themselves as such, by their numbers and by the variety and importance of the work they are doing they would force the straight world to accept them as colleagues and associates.

Possibly, but at this point we face a harsh reality. With certain exceptions an employer can legally fire an employee merely because he is gay. True, a handful of communities have enacted laws barring job discrimination on the basis of sexual preference, and a few governmental employers and some state-regulated industries are under orders not to discriminate in this fashion. And in theory there is protection for the gay employee working under a union contract, where it specifies just causes for discharge (which never include homosexuality).

Even these protections can be illusory. In almost any job, the employer can find some basis other than sexual preference for firing a gay employee. Work duties and requirements can be changed, sometimes very subtly, so that the gay employee finds the job intolerable and resigns. Or harassment by homophobic co-workers can force him to do the same thing.

Moreover, the effort and expense required to keep even a supposedly protected job can be ruinous. Unless the union will take up the gay member's cause, or some organization such as the American Civil Liberties Union will help, legal costs can be substantial. The proceedings may drag on for months, even years. If reinstatement to the job is finally ordered, the atmosphere at work is likely to be no less hostile than before.

The modest protections that exist today were unheard of twenty years ago, so there has been some improvement. Even so, the majority of gay men do not come out at work.

On the managerial and professional level, some employers still insist on a corporate conformity which includes a wife, children, and residence in a respectable suburb. However, many of them have backed off a bit in recent years, due not so much to gay liberation pressures as to changes in heterosexual lifestyles. Many younger straight men don't care for the conventional marriage relationship, and many young women choose to work rather than play the narrow, stereotyped role of corporate wife. So it is no longer as suspicious to be an unmarried male in the corporate and professional scene. While change has not been uniform, it is increasingly less necessary to engage in complex role-playing with talk of fictional heterosexual liaisons and the use of willing (or unsuspecting) female friends as dates for company social functions.

This makes it easy for fellow workers and employers to take the course of least resistance and ignore any indications that you are gay, short of your open announcement of the fact.

If you want to come out at work, consider the following checklist. The more questions you can answer with "yes," the better your prospects appear:

1. Is there another openly gay employee in a position comparable to yours? (This is a good sign, but it doesn't automatically mean you're safe; perhaps one homosexual is okay but two might start up fears that "*they* are trying to take over the place.")

2. Are promotions granted fairly to openly gay employees?
3. Do you work where laws or regulations forbid your employer from discriminating on the basis of sexual preference? Have you heard him express the intention to voluntarily comply with this ruling?
4. If you belong to a union, has it demonstrated equal enthusiasm in enforcing the rights of gay and straight employees under its contract?
5. Have your employer and co-workers openly expressed the belief that gay people should not be the subject of job discrimination?
6. Are you liked by your fellow employees?
7. Are you considered one of the more competent employees? Would your boss find it difficult to replace you with someone equally good?
8. Are a number of other jobs in your field readily available in your locality?

On the following questions, a "no" answer would be a good sign:

1. Have you actively misled your employer and co-workers into believing that you are heterosexual?
2. Have you been reprimanded for anything which could serve as a pretext for firing you, such as absenteeism or poor performance?
3. Have staff layoffs been rumored because business is slow?
4. Are co-workers blatantly hostile to gays? Are they obsessed with telling homophobic jokes?
5. Is your field one such as elementary school teacher or playground director, in which employment of gay people is considered to be controversial?
6. Is your employer highly religious and quite rigid about it, possibly the pillar of some fundamentalist, homophobic sect?

Obviously, the more positive answers you give to these last six questions, the more dangerous it would be to come out at work. Even a single yes suggests that the climate for personal revelations is full of risk.

In fact, if you feel a high level of homophobia in your work situation, you may be wise to start looking quietly for another job. Though you may not find one where you can be openly gay, at least you won't be working under the constant fear of being identified as homosexual.

As well, it could pay off in the future for you to give some thought now to what you might do if you got fired and were unable to get another job in your present field.

In the happy event that you *can* be open at work, don't get carried away. However sympathetic your employer and fellow employees may be, you're asking for trouble if you fool around on the job with other employees, and you're begging for it if you carry on with customers. This isn't discrimination, really, since such behavior by hetero-sexuals is equally frowned upon as being bad for business and as wasting company time. Usually it's a good idea to keep in mind the old adage that goes *Don't get your meat and your bread in the same store.*

Gay trades. The problem of coming out at work can be solved by finding employment in gay establishments or by entering one of the so-called "gay trades." These latter, though not always associated in the public mind with gay people, as a rule combine a high degree of job mobility with a minimum of employer or customer interest in the worker's private life.

Within the homosexual business scene the two principal jobs are those of bartender and steam bath attendant. For the former, youth and looks are a great help, often a require-ment, along with the ability to deal with the public. The money can be good, though more in tips than from salary, and it's a pleasant job for night people and outgoing types. On the other side of the coin the older gay bartender, however skilled, is less in demand, and two afflictions are endemic to this profession, alcoholism and varicose veins.

Bath attendants are paid little more than the minimum wage, and it isn't much of a job reference for the future. For many men it falls into the category of work taken until something better comes along. Still, it's a good way to learn the ins and outs of a lucrative business, and it beats unemployment.

Not every department store sales clerk is gay, nor every hairdresser or waiter, but these are certainly major gay trades. In the latter two occupations a man can do very well, like bartenders, from tips rather than salary. Pay is also low for clerks, who must dress well and do without gratuities. Most areas have an oversupply of men in all these lines of work, except for waitering.

The casting couch. This storied foundation of innumerable show business careers is not unknown in the gay world. You may have no moral objections to putting out in order to get a job, and your prospective employer may be attractive to you. Even so, ask yourself two questions: Will you have to continue having sex with the boss to keep the job? Will you lose your position the moment your employer gets interested in somebody else?

It's wise to think twice before you sign on the dotted divan.

Hustling as a career. As a rule, gay male prostitutes are not considered outcasts by other homosexuals, and as a practical matter legal problems can be avoided most of the time. Therefore, some young men think they can make good money by peddling their bodies. Well, it is possible, though not often on the street-hustler level. Whoring is a brief career, in a crowded and highly competitive field, and experience counts for less than youth. Also, selling one's sexual favors is a crime in most states; not much of one, often, but you do risk getting time in jail and your name in the papers.

Many a gay male prostitute, bright or dull, will say he is hustling only to get the big break. That is, Mr. Rich will come into his life one night, fall for him madly, and sweep him away to a life of culture, wealth, and ease. True, this does occur. It happens about as often as Halley's comet comes around, about once every seventy-six years.

Besides these drawbacks, hustling leads nowhere. The

smart man will hustle himself into something that has a future.

New fields. In choosing an agreeable kind of work, don't overlook occupations previously considered the exclusive province of females, such as secretarial work and nursing. Male employees are now often in demand because of governmental pressures to end sex discrimination in employment. Many heterosexual males still disdain these occupations, so employers frequently show small concern over the private lives of such men as do apply.

Because you will spend so much time at your job it is important not only to make the best choices of work you can, but also to decide how to deal with your sexual orientation in terms of your employment. Both matters demand a lot of careful thought; they will greatly influence your future happiness.

13 Medical Problems

Yield not to evils, but attack all the more boldly.
— Virgil

Gay men, because they tend to have more sex partners than do straights, are particularly exposed to infections and infestations that are transmitted by close bodily contact. As a man who loves men, you should be prepared to deal with a variety of conditions.

The crabs

Lice are a minor problem as such, but ridding yourself of them can seem an endless task if you are not completely thorough in your efforts. The proverbial dirty toilet seat can provide you with a case of what the French call the butterflies of love; but most often they're caught through sexual contact.

Three basic kinds of human lice will concern you, but only two of them are common. First is *Phthirus pubis*, the crab louse, sometimes known as the galloping freckle. It thrives in the genital region but can be found in most other hairy areas of the body, including legs, beard and moustache, and on rare occasions, in eyebrows and eyelashes.

Pediculus humanis capitis, or head louse, is second in popularity. It tends to form colonies around the ears and on the back of the head. This variety may venture as far south as the eyebrows but no further.

While pubic and head lice are not known to spread any diseases, *Pediculus corporis* (body louse) can be quite dangerous. It carries a number of illnesses including typhus. Fortunately, it is not common except in extremely unsanitary conditions such as trench warfare or among people who do not keep themselves clean. For most of us, *corporis* exposure is quite unlikely.

Any kind of lice can make you itch and play havoc with your social life; you'll want to banish them as soon as possible. Do not expect them to give up and go away on their own.

You should suspect lice if you develop an itch in any hairy part of your body, particularly the crotch, armpits, or head. Or, you might be plagued by sudden stinging bites from time to time. There may be nothing to see, or you may spot a number of dark spots, probably bluish, among the hairs. Possibly you will also notice tiny brown spots on your pillow, T shirt or underwear. If your case is well advanced, you might actually spot a louse or two, more easily with a magnifying glass. They usually lie on the skin, flat and unmoving, a dirty grey in color.

If you are suspicious but lack any graphic proof, try this: grasp a mass of hairs in the itchy area and pull outward; do this slowly and painlessly but firmly enough that loose or about-to-fall hairs will come free in your grip. Examine each strand carefully, perhaps with the help of a magnifier, especially down by the root. Is there a slightly oval offshoot hardly thicker than the strand of hair and about an eighth of an inch long? Does it stand at a distinct angle from the hair shaft? Blow on it; if it flies away, it's a bit of dust or dandruff. If it doesn't, its the nit (egg) of a louse.

You may find only one nit on many hairs, but no matter: consider yourself *infested*.

Here is what to do. Go to the drugstore and buy a bottle of parasiticide made especially to kill lice. A-200 Pyrinate, Li-Ban, Cuprex, Triple X, Rid, and Topicide are some of the better known brands, and all are non-prescription. Also, purchase a fine-toothed comb (sometimes called a rat-tail comb).

Apply the medication, carefully following the directions that accompany it. If pubic lice are the problem, medicate very widely, especially if you suspect you've been entertaining these guests for some time. Include all the hairy areas from the neck down to and including the toes, not forgetting the crack of your ass.

As pointed out earlier, pubic lice can flourish as high up as the eyebrows, which is the lower limit of head lice activity. If beard and moustache are lousy, shaving is the best idea. If brows or lashes are infested, you must go to a doctor. *Never put any lice remedies on your face;* you can lose your eyesight. Lice remedies are strong stuff and should be used as little as possible, anywhere on the body.

If you only have head lice, you need not treat any other part of the body.

After you wash off the medication, run the fine-toothed comb through the hairs of the affected area to remove nits and dead lice.

Now everything is fine. Or is it?

Without a warm body to cling to, lice can live for about twenty-four hours. The nits survive much longer, for up to fifteen days. The louse lays its eggs, often in great numbers, not only on your body hairs but also in your clothes. Washing or drycleaning will not necessarily get rid of the nits, which are stuck tightly in seams and interstices. Heat kills the eggs, but ironing clothes may not work because it's easy to miss a few nits here and there. And it just takes a couple to reinfest you. However nice and clean your pants may be, when you put them on your body warmth will hatch the nits, and the whole cycle will start over again. After all, a human being is merely a louse's means to create another louse.

This is what you must do, preferably before you medicate yourself: collect up all clothing and cloth material that has even a remote chance of being infested, and separate it into three piles — dirty laundry in one, clean clothes in another, and stuff that is very delicate or has to be drycleaned in a third.

The first pile you wash as usual. Then turn everything

inside out and put it into the dryer. Turn the dial to the hot-test setting and let the machine run for an hour. The idea is to toast the hell out of the nits.

The second group of clothes gets the same dryer treat-ment. The third pile should be set aside for at least fifteen days. Then it can be drycleaned as usual.

With lice it is better to overdo your clean-up efforts rather than let any possible source of infestation go untreated. While trying to get the crabs out of your life, consider such items as bedclothes, bathrobe, cloth bedroom slippers, bathroom rugs, towels, wash rags, toilet seat covers, laundry sack, stocking caps, mufflers, gloves, scarves; sportswear like jogging suits, jock straps, swim suits.

Thoroughly clean the bathroom, especially the toilet seat. When the problem is head lice, you will have to replace your brush and comb. Or you can boil them, but you might end up with a saucepan full of bubbling plastic.

Don't forget cloth-covered furniture, especially if you're accustomed to sit around in underwear or less, or like to sunbathe on a chaise longue.

And now you're done, right? Well. . . .

All your work will go for nothing if there are lice or nits on anyone who lives with you. Even for a roommate who has no signs, a bout of medication and the hot dryer treat-ment would be a very wise idea. Pets, fortunately, are less trouble than people. Cats and dogs can't get the kind of lice found on humans; only monkeys are susceptible.

It may be difficult to figure out when and where you picked up the lice, but do inform all your recent sexual contacts about this unfortunate development.

After ten days, check yourself carefully. If you find no signs, consider yourself free of the little devils at last.

That, believe it or not, is the easiest and most effective way to deal with lice. Alternative means might be useful in certain circumstances. Some men choose to shave their bodies. This does of course banish the nits (as long as the hairs are disposed of with care), but it's still wise to use a parasiticide as well. Nits in clothing can be killed by any thorough exposure to heat (at least 150° F. for at least 10 minutes) in the form of boiling water or live steam.

If you are highly allergic, suffer from skin reactions, or have any other kind of dermatitis, you should have your medication prescribed by a doctor and your treatment supervised by him.

Despite all your efforts you might find yourself reinfested. Repeat the whole procedure. If this doesn't work, you may want to have a doctor prescribe some extra-potent parasiticide such as Kwell.

There are several things that should not be done, no matter how desperate you may get. You may have heard of the old home remedy of soaking clothes in kerosene and of applying it (mixed fifty-fifty with vegetable oil) to the body. Kerosene can burn the skin, it's toxic, inflammable, gives off dangerous fumes, and it reeks. It's likely to ruin even slightly delicate clothing. In short, since safe, cheap medications are easily available, kerosene is a bad idea.

Even worse, absolutely unthinkable in fact, is to use commercial insecticides on your clothes or body. A friend of ours, who panicked at discovering that he was not alone, applied roach spray to his crotch area. He quickly became quite ill, had to be hospitalized, and remains genitally bald to this day.

Scabies

This is the fabled seven-year itch or, more commonly, merely the itch. You will never see the tiny creature that causes it, and it's unlikely that you'll figure out where you picked it up because the symptoms take a month or so to develop. You can be reasonably sure, though, that your exposure came from close bodily contact.

Basically, you are being used as a hatchery by the mite *Sarcoptes scabiei*. The female tunnels into your skin, just under the surface, and leaves eggs as she goes. They hatch, come up for air, then re-enter you via a hair follicle to breed some more.

All this activity gives you certain characteristic symptoms. You itch like mad, for one, and you may find one or more dark, hairlike lines on your skin. In addition, or instead, you may discover numerous red "flea bites" on your body. Fortunately, scabies rarely attacks above the neck.

Wrists, spaces between fingers, elbows, lower abdomen, buttocks, and thighs are the preferred areas.

Because the medication that will kill scabies has to be powerful enough to sink into your skin (Kwell and Eurax are most often used), it must be prescribed by a doctor. Given the intensity of the itching, it's doubtful that anyone would hesitate to seek treatment, but if scabies is neglected, all kinds of unpleasant skin problems can start up.

Be sure your recent sex partners (within five weeks before discovery) are informed and get treatment. You need not fret over every bit of clothing, however; scabies is very contagious, but only through intimate contact. The mites do not live in clothes.

Heat intensifies the itching. Until the treatment takes effect, keep baths and showers lukewarm. And finally, if you get both scabies and lice at the same time, the medications used for the scabies will also do away with the lice.

Intestinal parasites

Weight loss, diarrhea that gets worse and worse, pains in the gut, and fever — these are the well-known symptoms of what is variously called travelers' trots, Delhi belly, the gleet, turista, and Montezuma's revenge.

No longer must you journey to distant lands to pick up such illnesses as amebiasis, giardiasis, or shigellosis. In the United States these bacterial and protozoal diseases are on the rise among gay men. In a recent year the San Francisco Department of Health reported a nearly three hundred per cent increase in cases of amebiasis.

These parasites spread via fecal material. Unwashed hands can give them to you in a restaurant, and of course they can pass from one man to another during the close contact of sex. This is especially easy with the more uninhibited, anally oriented kinds of carrying-on. The creatures may live quietly in your colon and cause no symptoms at all. Then, irritated into multiplying feverishly (by a night of heavy drinking, for instance), they suddenly make their presence known.

Sometimes the condition is not all that dramatic in its presentation. You may have nothing more than slight bouts of the trots from time to time, an occasional day of malaise and small appetite, or an unusual sensation of gas rumbling around in your guts.

If you are sure you have some kind of intestinal bug, or if you think you might, get checked out by a doctor, and don't depend on cures from the drugstore or folk remedies. If not diagnosed and properly dispatched, these parasites can spread to the liver, kidneys, even lungs, places where they can do you a great deal of harm.

Inform your recent sex partners of your condition, and remember that the best prevention is cleanliness.

Gonorrhea

The clap is the most common venereal disease among gay men. Once it is outside the body the gonococcus dies rather quickly, so it is almost impossible to pick up a dose from that infamous dirty toilet seat. The nearly inevitable means of transmission is by direct sexual contact.

It is understandable, but incorrect, to think that the clap is a disease of the sex organs. In truth it is an infection that strikes mucous membranes. Thus, in addition to the urethral passage in the penis, it can thrive in the rectum, the throat, or even the eyes.

The first sign may be a gooey, whitish to yellowish discharge coming from the infected area. If this is the penis, the urethral opening will probably sting or burn, especially during urination. (Many men first realize something is wrong when they discover odd stains on undershorts or pajamas.) In the throat the symptoms usually give a good imitation of the common cold. Eye infection is marked by irritation, tears, and perhaps some pus. Rectal soreness can become so great that it is difficult to walk, and there may be a constant feeling of needing to have a bowel movement. White, fuzzy lines may appear on the feces, and defecation may begin with a spurt of thick, yellowish pus.

Sometimes gonorrhea creates no symptoms at all, and you will find out about this kind only when a sex partner tells you the bad news. This is especially true of anal and oral clap.

Most usually, gonorrhea strikes in the penis and rectum, with the throat being a distant third. Rarely is it found in the eyes, which is good, because that is an exceedingly dangerous location.

You may have heard, perhaps as locker room talk, that the clap is not serious and that it will go away. Yes, the visible symptoms will eventually clear up. However, if the clap is left untreated it can cause a lot of damage. The penis especially can be affected, lessening your pleasure (and sometimes your performance) during sex, and making urination anything but easy. After a while gonorrhea can spread in the form of arthritis. And eye infection can quickly lead to impaired vision or blindness.

These complications are rare today because the disease can be easily, quickly treated. When you think you have gonorrhea, go to your doctor or to the local health department or public health clinic.

Treatment is by penicillin. For five to ten days afterwards you should avoid any kind of sex including masturbation, so the inflamed tissues will have a chance to heal. It's a good idea as well to avoid coffee, booze, or spicy foods.

You may have heard horror stories about a strain of gonorrhea that's incurable. Certain kinds of clap are not affected by penicillin, true, but some other kind of antibiotic will do the job.

Inform your sex partners as soon as you know what you have. Symptoms appear two to eight days after exposure, with three to five days being quite usual and ten days the outside limit. (In the eyes symptoms may appear as soon as twelve hours after exposure.) Be especially sure to inform any married men you've had sex with and (if you're bisexual or experimenting) any women. Gonorrhea is often undetectable in females and can cause a good deal of harm; sterility is a common result.

For as long as you are infectious, take great care to keep your hands clean, especially if you wear contact lenses.

Nonspecific urethritis (NSU)

Also known as nongonococcal urethritis (NGU), this is a bacterial infection of the penis (and rectum) with symptoms almost identical to those of the clap. Once again, the most common mode of transmission is by sexual activity. NSU symptoms may clear by themselves in a few weeks, but Chlamydia, the bacterium that is the cause of the disease, can do damage to your plumbing or lead to other complications. So it's good to clear it up, which is easily accomplished with antibiotics and abstention from sex for a while.

Because strictly speaking this is not a venereal disease, and because of their limited budgets, most public health clinics will not treat this condition but will refer you to your private doctor.

Syphilis

This is one of the most treacherous and horrible diseases known, and until the discovery of penicillin it was exceedingly difficult to cure or control. The writer Guy de Maupassant died raving in an insane asylum because of syphilis; Oscar Wilde's end came as a result of syphilis of the brain. The composer Gaetano Donizetti began screaming at an opera rehearsal one day, lost his reason, suffered from uncontrollable sex desires for a time, then died after several years as a vegetable, barely able to recognize his old friends or his own music.

Today this disease is so little dreaded that many people believe it to be a rarity that they don't have to worry about.

Do not fool yourself. Syphilis is still a problem, especially because you may not notice when you get it and years may pass before gross symptoms show, by which time severe or even fatal damage has been done.

This is what happens: during the close physical contact, as in sex, the bacterium *Treponema pallidum* passes into the body through any tiny lesion or nick. In ten days or so a painless, infectious, slow-to-heal "pimple" or "flea bite" may develop. Innocent looking, or occurring where it is not visible, inside the penis canal or in the rectum, it easily passes unnoticed. This is primary syphilis.

A month or two later the syphilis victim may feel rather blah, aching, slightly feverish, with a noticeable skin eruption and an unusual amount of hair loss. These symptoms may or may not all appear; perhaps none of them will show. (Syphilis is nothing if not tricky.) At the worst they will clear up in a week or two. All this time the person with the disease is highly infectious, and will remain so for about a year. That's secondary syphilis.

Then, for years, nothing happens. *Treponema* quietly tends to its business, never disturbing any of the body's alarm systems, going on thus for up to two or three decades, perhaps for the rest of a long lifetime. However, it may attack almost any part of the body, and it favors the heart and nervous system (Donizetti thought his terrible headaches were just migraines), causing debility, insanity, and death.

Thanks to penicillin this tertiary stage of syphilis is rare. Even so, the sexually active gay man should take great care to watch for this disease.

If you find a suspicious pimple on your body, especially in the genital-rectal area, or if you suddenly develop a skin rash or a mass of pimples, then you should promptly get a blood test at the health department or from your doctor.

Signs or no, it is smart to be checked for syphilis at least once a year, and preferably more often. First of all, there is no immunity to this disease; you can get it over and over again. Second, blood tests are not always accurate. This month you might get negative results, and six weeks from now they might show as positive, even without any exposure in between. Finally, the signs of syphilis are not always obvious, and when they are it's easy to mistake them for something unimportant or overlook them altogether.

The usual treatment for syphilis is a dose of penicillin, injected into the buns.

If you get syphilis, of course you must inform every person you could possibly have exposed. If you don't know where you picked it up, and that's something you probably won't be able to figure out, then get an estimate of how long you've been infected from the medical people who are treating you. Then be sure to contact everyone you can reach, even if that means locating a year's worth of sex partners.

Syphilis is no longer the worldwide scourge it once was, and gonorrhea may be more of a drag than a danger, but neither can safely be neglected. You can take some precautions to reduce the danger of contracting these diseases, particularly the clap.

You can use a condom (a rubber) during anal sex. These rather comical devices are not popular among gay men since they somewhat deaden feeling. You can get around that by using skins. These are condoms made of animal intestines; being flesh, they heat quickly to body temperature and are less noticeable during use. Fourex is a commonly available brand. They do have drawbacks: skins dry out and get hard if not kept wet in their containers, and they're more expensive than regular rubbers.

If rubbers are out of the question for you, consider the pro kit. This item was issued by the millions to servicemen during World War II but since then has slipped into obscurity. It is still available, though, as the Dough-Boy Prophylactic or the Sanitube. Simply, the pro kit is a little container of calomel (mercurous chloride). Within two hours after sex you squeeze some of the contents up your urethra, following directions on the packet, and spread the rest on the outside of the penis.

The makers of pro kits mention nothing about anal use. Several gay friends say they work as well in back as in front. However, the rectum absorbs matter into the bloodstream, so calomel has a chance of being toxic if used anally.

The medication is left in place for several hours, then expelled from within and washed off the skin.

There are gay men who swear by pro kits, and not much can be said against their use except that calomel is fairly allergenic and that giving yourself a pro is a rather clinical finale to a bout of love or a night at the baths. (It is true that calomel is a derivative of that notorious poison, mercury, but with proper use it is harmless. Drug reference books list the substance as having no appreciable side effects. Well, there is one: do not attempt to dose your throat with the contents of a pro kit; calomel is ferociously laxative.)

Handy as they are, pro kits are not always easy to find. Pharmacies in middle- or upper-class neighborhoods rarely seem to stock them. Where available they are never on display; you have to ask for them. Try a drug store that is downtown or in a less genteel area of your city. They can be ordered direct from the manufacturer; see the bibliography.

Finally, whatever other precautions you take to keep from getting VD, always try to urinate as soon as possible after sex, then wash yourself very thoroughly, using lots of soap and hot water. You can take advantage of soap's mild antiseptic effect by working some mushy bits of it down into your urethra.

Hepatitis

Among the viral diseases most common among gay men, this infirmity of the liver is the worst of the lot. It is spread by oral-fecal contact, principally, but also by body fluids such as saliva, urine, semen, and blood. Obviously, sex is a great way to get hepatitis.

There are three varieties. Type A (infectious) is the most common form among straights, and takes two to six weeks to appear. Type B (serum) is less prevalent in the general population than is type A, but more common among gay men and more dangerous. It shows up six weeks to six months after exposure. A third kind of hep has recently been recognized. Informally dubbed type C, it too is often found in gay men, and not much is known about it.

Whatever the type, hepatitis will make you feel terrible — incredibly fatigued, without appetite, probably nauseated and feverish. After a few days you will begin to feel relatively better, though still terribly tired. About this time your urine will turn dark brown and your feces will get pale or even white and your skin and eyes will take on an ugly yellow color.

It is possible to have hepatitis without realizing it. A light attack may pass as a case of the flu or merely as no more than a day or two of the blahs.

Rest is the best cure for hepatitis, usually several months' worth, along with good food, vitamins, and careful avoidance of anything that puts a strain on your sick liver, like alcohol, drugs, or fatty foods. Though little more can be done, medical attention is important in case any complications develop or if you in reality have some other liver condition, one that produces hepatitis-like symptoms.

You can get each type of hepatitis only once, but having had one type gives no protection from getting the others. If you have been exposed to type A hepatitis, a gamma globulin shot is a good idea.

Once more, if you get the hep, inform anybody you may have infected. For type A, figure that you could have passed it on to sex partners for ten days before you get sick, and assume that you're contagious as long as you're deathly ill. You are probably contagious with type B before you know you have it and you may still be contagious for the duration of the worst of your illness. Medical research has not yet settled this question.

With type B you may remain a carrier all your life. Your doctor can test you to see if you are or not.

At this writing a vaccine is being developed for use against type B hepatitis. When it is available, gay men should be among the first to take advantage of its protection.

Herpes

Also known as fever blisters, herpes simplex can appear at many locations on your body. Since it can spread by sexual activity, the penis and anus are favored spots. The itchy, painful little bumps of clear fluid will dry up, form a crust and after three weeks or so they'll disappear.

Herpes can recur time and again, and no cure is known, although several treatments are in the experimental stage. It sometimes clears up on its own but possibly not until after a number of attacks. You can do little but treat the affected areas for pain, keep them as dry as possible, and stay on the alert for secondary infections.

Venereal warts

A new growth on the penis or anywhere in the anal-genital area should be examined by a doctor — it may be a sign of syphilis. Usually it's found to be something far less dangerous: venereal (or genital) warts. Like hepatitis and herpes they're caused by a virus, are contagious, and can be passed via sex. They tend to persist and recur. Gay men who enjoy anal sex may suffer them around or within the rectum, where their presence can make sexual activity quite painful.

There is no effective drugstore remedy for venereal warts; they have to be removed by a doctor. Usually this is an office procedure.

The time between exposure and development may be as much as six months but can be far less. Tell all your intimate contacts who might have been exposed.

Scrapes and aches

Sex between men can get rather rough-and-tumble. Alone or in combination, such things as booze, grass, some other drugs, and sheer ecstasy can induce a certain amount of anesthesia in the body. So keep an eye on all appreciable scratches, love-bites, and the like. Get to a doctor right away if you find any pronounced redness of the skin, warmth, a throbbing sensation, or signs of pus. This is especially important for injuries caused by the mouth, well known as the dirtiest orifice in the body.

Though ordinary anal sex commonly does not lead to problems in the rectum, fistfucking can be dangerous and so can the use of dildoes. Rough play, careless insertion or withdrawal, and insufficient lubrication may cause damage. The colon has no way to register pain, so you may not feel any immediate signs of injury. Indications of internal difficulties include sudden fever, a crampy feeling or acutely painful gut-ache, and of course blood coming from the rectum (on feces or by itself). *Get medical attention at once.*

Getting medical help

As a gay man you may hesitate to seek treatment, fearing to reveal certain facts about yourself and others. This of course is especially the case when the condition is venereal and its location is rectal. This problem is not as great as it may seem.

When you think you have the clap or syphilis, you have the choice between a private doctor and the local VD clinic. Roughly speaking, the more you have to lose and the smaller your community, the better it is to see a doctor. Of course it is best to find one who is gay (see Chapter 18) or at least worldly.

Physicians are normally required to report all confirmed cases of venereal disease to health authorities. But even if you have anal clap, you need say nothing; the doctor is not likely to ask embarrassing questions. Not every case of VD gets reported, especially where a physician knows the patient personally or has been his doctor for some time or doesn't want to bother with the paperwork. Even so, it is best to be extremely cautious about requesting him to not comply with the law.

The public health clinic has the big disadvantage, for some people, of being public and the little disadvantage of being time-consuming. (The same can be said for the free clinic, still found in some cities.) But there is little or no charge for its services, it functions quite effectively, and no judgments are made on anyone's lifestyle.

In some areas the clinic may be open for only a day or two during the week, but in many cities they operate from Monday through Friday. They keep usual daytime hours, as a rule, and often stay open at night once or twice a week.

Telephone to find out the schedule, and don't panic if you can't go in right away; another day or two of VD won't be fatal (except for gonorrhea in the eyes, which requires treatment at once). Just don't have any sex in the meantime.

If you can, visit the clinic as soon as it opens. The crowds come later, so you can get everything over with faster if you go early. You might want to bring something to read during waits.

What should you expect at a VD clinic? You register and receive a number; as in steambaths you'll be paged by it, never by your name. You then wait in the lounge until a health worker calls your number and takes you to a private room. There he or she will get some vital statistics and ask about your sexual contacts — who exposed you and whom you may have exposed.

You can be reasonably sure than any information you give will never go beyond the health department's files. You can identify your recent sex partners, and the worker or someone else will contact them in the near future, without bringing your name into the situation. If you prefer you can be vague, giving a story of some passing adventure. In this case, of course, *you* must take full responsibility for contacting everyone you may have exposed to VD.

If you're going to tell the health worker anything, tell everything, and bring names and addresses or phone numbers. Don't worry that he or she will become outraged or faint dead away in shock and horror. The health worker has heard it all, and if you can manage to dumbfound any clinic employee you should get a door prize.

More time in the waiting room, and then you will have a brief, private consultation with a doctor. He will ask you to drop your pants so he can get a smear of any discharge, or so he can check out the suspicious pimple. When pus is coming from the penis he will ask you to milk a little of it onto a glass slide. If the infection is rectal, he will have you bend over and spread your cheeks while he takes a sample with a swab. And he will use a swab for problems in the throat.

The slide will be taken away for examination, which requires only a few minutes. If the doctor says you do indeed have the clap or syphilis, now is the time for you to speak up if you are allergic to penicillin. In all likelihood you will have been questioned about this already, but if not, be *sure* to mention it.

With a sigh you return again to the lounge. When your number is next called, it will be for treatment. Injection is more probable than capsules with gonorrhea and inevitable in treating syphilis.

Now you're done. Sometimes, though, you are asked to stay in the waiting room for another twenty minutes or so, in case you develop a penicillin reaction.

If, in the first half-hour or so after you have been treated you begin to feel weak, dizzy, nauseated, or otherwise suddenly and generally terrible, you're probably having a reaction. Return at once to the clinic, or if that's not possible, go to the nearest medical facility.

When you get treatment for gonorrhea, you might be given a blood test too. At some places it's voluntary or has to be requested. It's a good idea, and since you're at the clinic anyway it won't even take much time. A blood sample is drawn from a vein in the crook of your arm, and that's it. You don't have to wait for laboratory results; if any sign of syphilis is found, you are notified by mail or telephone.

We have been repetitious about the need to tell your sex partners they've been exposed to something because many men new to the gay world are shy about doing so. You may not believe it, but most gay men you contact with the bad news will thank you politely for the information.

Among homosexuals who lead active sex lives, it is common to keep a list of bed partners. This can be done with almost no effort. Hold on to all the trick cards (calling cards) and all the cocktail napkins, matchbook covers, and the like on which phone numbers are scribbled. On each artifact write the date of the contact, then stow the bit of paper in a desk drawer, and you have a file that could come in handy.

Keeping track in this or some more formal way is a tiny price to pay for an active sex life and good health. Remember too that the more careless or indifferent you are, the more people will spread your infection, and the more likely it is to get back to you again in the near future, and again and again.

PSYCHOLOGICAL PROBLEMS

Physical health

Sometimes, when a man becomes sexually active with other men, the first time he comes down with one of the conditions we have described he also suffers a terrible feeling of guilt. He feels that God or Fate is punishing him for his sexual "wickedness." If this happens to you, the unpleasant feeling will often vanish once you consider the facts of your situation: these infestations and infections are the result of physical intimacy, nothing more. They're an unfortunate side of sexual activity, and that's all. A man can live in fear of some Higher Power who is waiting to fire a lightning bolt full of clap at his cock or ass, but it's better to be practical in dealing with what are essentially nothing more than inconveniences. Know the signs and symptoms, care for any medical problems promptly and effectively, and have frequent physical checkups.

Mental Health

The process of coming out can be quite rough and stressful. Head problems can develop, or those already present can get worse. Individual circumstances and resources vary so widely that each man must bc his own judge. Remember that tensions can mount slowly and insidiously, and keep on the watch for these common danger signals of rising and excessive stress:

- Problems with sleeping.
- Sudden loss of appetite, or intense craving for food.
- Indifference to personal appearance and hygiene.
- A sudden interest in alcohol or drugs, or an abrupt increase in their use.
- Withdrawal from usual relationships and activities.
- Feelings of inability to cope, or a sense of being immobilized, on the job or in school.
- Sudden and unusual mood changes, instant rages, plunges into acute depression.
- Long-term or chronic feelings of unhappiness, such as an unshakeable melancholy, a strong sense of self-loathing or unworthiness or inferiority, a continuing state of fearfulness and anxiety.
- Persistent thoughts of suicide.
- A pattern of self-destructive impulses such as several car accidents within a short space of time, impulsive chance-taking with the excuse of "just showing off," or getting into brawls.

To grasp your problems clearly, often it's enough to talk them out with a sympathetic friend. However, at a time of great tension or crisis a trained, neutral observer may be of more value. Sometimes only a few sessions of counseling are needed, but frequently the process of unraveling head problems can take more time.

Though the attitude is slowly dying out, in all walks of life some people still reject any form of mental therapy. Some feel that by accepting it they define themselves as crazy. The truth is that psychotherapy works best with those who are merely troubled and is often ineffective in helping the outright psychotic. Others fear psychotherapy as a form of brainwashing. Even with the most skilled practitioner and the most cooperative patient, it is by no means so efficient. Diabolic mindfucks (and overnight cures as well) exist only in old movies.

Information about therapy resources in your area can be obtained from the health department, free clinic, gay health organization, gay raps, publications, or information lines. And don't let the expense scare you off. Students may be able to arrange cheap or free sessions at their college or university. Some counseling set-ups operate on a sliding-scale basis, charging fees according to ability to pay. Many employee health plans have provisions for covering a share of therapy expenses.

Privacy is not difficult to maintain. Therapists generally keep their notes in code and are extremely reluctant to make them public, even under subpoena. Where some of the costs are borne by a health plan at work, it is illegal for the insurance carrier to pass on the information to the employer. And the various personal problems a person may have are represented by code numbers in the insuror's paperwork. Here again the psychotherapist's discretion comes into play: he is very likely to describe your difficulties with some catch-all like "anxiety."

Generally speaking, the advisor most able to help and understand a gay man will be gay himself. When you have a choice of resources you will usually be wisest to go to a gay-sponsored one for the help you need.

AIDS

About 1980 a number of previously rare diseases began to appear in people who were mostly younger gay men. Since then the cause has been discovered to be a mysterious breakdown of the body's natural defense system. This is acquired immune deficiency syndrome, AIDS for short.

Both psychologically and medically, AIDS creates a number of problems for the gay man. Homophobic straights have used the situation as an excuse to justify discrimination (and worse) against gays. And gay men must work out ways of having a satisfying sex life without ruining their health and endangering their lives.

At this writing no cure for AIDS is known. However, statistically speaking, the chances of getting AIDS are not great. Cases number only a few thousand, including non-gay victims, and there are an estimated fifteen million gay men in North America. The exact method of transmission has not yet been established, but it's clear that more than casual contact is required. It appears likely that an exchange of body fluids is necessary: semen, blood, or possibly saliva.

Until more is learned about AIDS, gay men should avoid anonymous sex or sex with a number of partners. Orgy rooms in baths and back rooms in bars are out for the duration. It's wise to know your playmates beforehand so you can avoid the fast-lane I-don't-care types. Indulge in the kinds of sex which don't involve passing body fluids. For any kind of penetration, a condom should be used. Finally, keep an eye on the press for news on the latest developments in knowledge about AIDS.

It is to be hoped that medical research will soon relegate AIDS to the history books. Neither acquired immune deficiency syndrome, while it lasts, nor any other problem gives you an excuse to neglect your health. This means exercising due caution in your sex life and dealing with small problems, medical or psychological, before they become huge ones.

14 Recreational Drug Use

The delight that consumes the desire,
The desire that outruns the delight.

— Swinburne

Taking drugs for the pleasure they give has grown more
common in the United States in recent years, and in gay
scenes you will run into drug use often. Whether such
activity interests you personally or not, it's good to know
something about it.

Speaking generally, gay male preferences in dope are
extensively influenced by a preoccupation with sex and by
the existence of a highly developed social structure. True
dope addiction of the heroin-morphine school is rarely seen
within the gay world for two reasons. First, extended opiate
use often causes impotence. Second, the high cost of the
stuff forces the user into an "addictive personality" lifestyle.
While this may attract marginal types who feel they are
adrift in a formless universe, it has little appeal to the gay
man. His own social structure is more comfortable and
satisfying, and it may even exert useful pressures. Once a
man is known to be shooting up ("I'm just skin-popping
once in a while, that's all"), his friends drop him, well
aware that sooner or later he'll try to rip them off.

Such established dope subculture as exists in gay life
usually does not involve intense concentration on one kind

of drug, but rather is a matter of the frequent but still recreational use of a variety of drugs.

Dope as a way of life is rejected by most gay men, but it is employed, sometimes rather extensively, as a diversion in itself and as a complement to the sex act.

Drugs go in and out of fashion, like anything else; one thing will be popular here, unheard-of there, and passé somewhere else. These substances are generally the most common:

Marijuana. Everybody's favorite high is quite popular among gay men, especially for its quality of sensuous relaxation. It is much enjoyed in the bedroom. Grass is common in steam baths, and many a guy goes to the bars stoned. Even where the authorities are lenient, it's still considered a little tacky to smoke weed inside a bar. But often several patrons will retire to the nearest alley to toke up. In one of our favorite drinking places, the custom on returning from such an errand is to present the roach to the bartender.

The cumulative effects of marijuana smoking are the subject of much exaggeration and controversy, but it is clear that a joint can carry as much unhealthy tar and nicotine as two cigarettes.

There are other minor drawbacks. With steady use, grass can dull one's memory a bit, but the effect seems to be reversed merely by no longer smoking. (Incessant use all day long, day after day, of maybe thirty to forty joints can create a stuporous condition called burnout, but this is a problem confined to a few teenagers who think it's the hip thing to do since they're failing woodshop anyway.) Otherwise, marijuana may present a problem for people who are in therapy. Smoked a lot, or around bedtime, weed has the effect of suppressing dreams, or at least one's memory of the dreams.

Sometimes a concentrated form of marijuana, THC, is supposedly sold in the street. Forget it. Real THC is difficult to manufacture, hard to keep in its potent state, and expensive. What's being sold is probably a lot more harmful than any marijuana derivative.

Grass is not addicting.

Amyl nitrite. Also isoamyl nitrite, butyl nitrite, isobutyl nitrite, and, incorrectly but commonly, amyl ni*trate.* This is the inhalant especially favored by gay men, its several varieties collectively referred to as poppers or amyl.

Originally the liquid was sealed inside delicate glass ampules encased in gauze cocoons. These were broken (or popped) so the contents could be inhaled, thus relieving the agony of an angina pectoris attack.

Amyl relaxes the smooth muscle tissues in the body, which means that when it's sniffed one's veins dilate. This causes a drop in blood pressure, which panics the heart into overdrive; a surge of blood sweeps through one's body, including the brain. All this action induces an odd sensation, a combination of both a distinct euphoria and a feeling of having just been fired from a cannon.

The effect lasts a few minutes at most, which, all things considered, is fortunate.

Why should heart cases have all the fun, somebody asked long ago. (The recreational, if not sexual, use of amyl is mentioned in *Quartet,* a Jean Rhys novel published in 1928.) But poppers didn't catch on widely for a long time, not until the 1960s when they were taken up by many gay men and a few straights.

It is said that the principal supplier of amyl, the staid pharmaceutical firm of Burroughs-Wellcome, was shocked to learn that its product was being used for fun in bed. Amyl nitrite suddenly became a prescription medication.

It didn't do much good. Poppers are not hard to manufacture. In most states arrests or harassment for its non-medical use are virtually nonexistent. Even so, the precaution is often taken of offering the stuff for sale as a room odorizer. Well, amyl works fine for that, if you like your room to smell like well-used gym socks.

Amyl is sold in adult book stores, in many gay bars and baths, and by mail order. Usually it is a clear or yellowish liquid that vaporizes at room temperature, sold in little brown flasks. The ampule form is sometimes available despite Burroughs-Wellcome's unsporting attitude, and recently amyl in solid form has come on the market.

Because it is so volatile, amyl is best stored in the freezer.

Keep it away from long exposure to light, which causes a breakdown of the chemical.

Heavy exposure to volatile nitrites can cause a kidney disease called methemoglobinemia, but so far there are no reports in medical literature of any great harm resulting from the use of poppers. Some cautions are in order, however. Amyl is not a good idea for anyone with heart trouble (unless prescribed by a doctor, but that isn't done much any more), circulatory problems, asthma, emphysema, or any other kind of pulmonary difficulty. It is not recommended for use by anyone with glaucoma. Any stroke victim who does poppers must be insane or suicidal.

An occasional person has an allergic reaction to amyl, but serious difficulties of this sort are rare.

At discos and dance halls, if you are breathless, hyperventilating, boozed up, or stoned on grass, a sniff of poppers can make you faint dead away. Physical injury such as a concussion or broken teeth is a possibility.

In the bedroom amyl nitrite can do much to make sex exceedingly wild and abandoned, but keep two things in mind. First, the liquid can cause skin burns, especially to mucous membranes, and it can seriously damage the eyes. However mad the action, you must not slop poppers around. Many gay men use an aluminum inhaler called a bullet. These cost a few dollars where poppers are sold.

Second, during ecstatic sex it is easy to hurt yourself or your partner without realizing it, because your pain sensation is lessened. Don't let poppers (or any other substance or any combination of them) break your contact with mission control.

Two minor considerations: Poppers sometimes spoil the fun by causing a temporary loss of erection. Men who react thus either avoid using amyl or limit their inhalations to a few moments before ejaculation. Second, anyone who favors sex by candlelight should be aware that liquid amyl is quite flammable.

There is only one way to do poppers, and that is by breathing the fumes into the lungs via nose or mouth. In liquid form amyl is poisonous; drinking it is extremely dangerous (and useless as well: gastric secretions decompose the chemical structure of poppers), and anal intake is even more so. Shooting up with it is worse yet. Don't experiment; the results can be fatal.

Since a tolerance may develop with repeated exposure, decreasing the effect, many gay men do poppers only when they are having sex. Amyl can be overdone, although it isn't easy to manage this. If you feel dragged-out all day, you may be using it excessively.

Amyl, in any of its forms, is not addictive.

Downers. Principally these are the barbiturates and such tranquilizers as Valium. Because they make the user dreamy and calm and very often non-erect, they are not remarkably popular among gay men. Methaqualone is the exception, better known by such brand names as Quaalude, Mequin, Parest, and Sopor, and on the street as 'ludes, love drug, quackers, seven-fourteens, quads, sopes, and wall-bangers. Usually found in tablet form, they induce a floating sort of state that's accompanied by a strong interest in having sex. (This apparent aphrodisiac effect may occur because problems and anxieties are suppressed, leaving one's head and body free to concentrate on erotic matters.)

Charming, but.... With drugs there's always a but and with this one there are two: first, hot and bothered as you may feel, getting and staying hard is by no means assured; second, doing 'ludes all the time can be very rough on your liver.

Barbiturates are addictive. Valium is not, but it can create a strong psychological dependence. Without exception, all downers are dangerous in combination with alcohol. The formula is, booze plus downers equals coma. If it's deep enough the heart will stop, and we all know what comes after that.

Speed. Anything that makes you awake, alert, and lively may be called speed, but the term applies mainly to the amphetamines (Methedrine, Benzedrine, Dexamed, Dexedrine, etc.). It's handy if you want to dance and party all weekend long, but the effects otherwise vary greatly. Amphetamines can put you in a rather low-down sexy mood and shrivel the dick at the same time. While some (usually quite young) men can get it up on speed, among them are guys who then have trouble going soft again. This may sound like anything but bad news, but a sore and aching erect penis is no treat.

When the sex act is possible, the participants are often left feeling unsatisfied no matter what or how much they do.

An allegedly more reliable kind of speed for sex is the fabled cocaine, not an amphetamine but a derivative of the coca plant. It lifts the spirits with a subtle intensity. The major effect may last only half an hour or so, but a calm, pleasant afterglow may continue for some hours.

There are several problems with speed. Benzedrines and such put a terrible strain on the body, ("Hey, this stuff is great! I've been up since a week ago Friday, and I don't feel tired at all!"), and whatever is weakest is most likely to be the first thing to break down. Especially prone are the heart, the liver, the circulatory system, and the brain. At the least, prolonged use leaves muscles and tissues overworked and sagging, and the speed-freak typically has a haggard, lined, prematurely aged look.

Cocaine, sniffed as a powder, destroys mucous membranes, so the long-time user will end up with a nice hole in his nasal septum.

Amphetamines are addictive. For a long time cocaine was thought not to be, but now there is evidence to the contrary. Coke's defenders reject this, but the question of addiction is of little importance when the substance creates a very strong psychological dependence in the user. As the late actress Tallulah Bankhead is supposed to have said, "Of course coke's not addicting. I should know, dahling, I've been using it for years."

Psychedelics/Hallucinogens. LSD (lysergic acid diethylamide) is the principal substance in this category, and commonly is called acid. Some men like to frequent discos and bars while blissed to the eyeballs, and others enjoy the curious here-but-not-here effect that acid has when mixed with sex. However, you are playing risky games with your head when you take acid frequently.

Acid is best taken in an environment that makes the tripper feel safe and secure, with someone else around who can handle any problems that come up.

Among gay men LSD use is common but not frequent, for the most part.

Acid is not addictive. Neither are similar substances such as mescalin and psylocibin.

Deadly body rotters. So much hysterical nonsense and outright lies have been written about drugs that many people suspect no drug can be as bad as it's painted. Well, there are some compounds that you can do without, even once.

At the most primitive teenage (and sometimes disco) level is the practice of sniffing glue, paint thinner, and the like. The high is brief, and it doesn't take much use to wreck the brain.

The real champion in grey-matter destruction must be PCP (phencyclidine), also known as angel dust, monkey dust, peace pill, goon, crystal, hog, rocket fuel, surfer, K-J, or skag. It is usually sold as a water-soluble powder and can be taken in many ways. If a joint you smoke has a lettuce taste to it, it has probably been laced with PCP.

The effect can be a nice, airy high, but freakouts are common and frequently include behavior that ranges from bizarre to psychotic, with results that sometimes are homicidal, self-mutilating, or suicidal. Many a PCP freakout has been diagnosed in emergency wards as an acute episode of schizophrenia. And the stuff can cause flashbacks, later reactions to a dose which come on without warning. Between doses users often face a terrible depression-anxiety state, so they feel compelled to continue taking the drug. Though there is no certainty yet, it appears the lengthy use of PCP can severely dull mental function.

MDA (methylenedioxyamphetamine) is one of the strongest kinds of speed, and it has psychedelic effects in addition. This may sound like a charming combination, but

MDA is harsh on the liver; there are strong suspicions that it can literally cause hepatitis.

All these substances, including glue and thinner, are addictive, along with such similar street drugs as DOM and DMT (STP).

Buying drugs. If you're going to buy dope, know your dealer. Be sure he is established in the community and has a lot to lose if he peddles bad stuff. Do not score from strangers on the street or in the men's room at the disco. That way you'll probably get burned, if not poisoned.

Street drugs are manufactured in laboratories that are secret, probably jerry-built, and run by people who may hardly know or care what they are doing beyond making a buck. One substance can be passed off as another. Impure chemicals and sloppy processes may have considerable effect on the final product. Once again, if you must have drugs, know your dealer. There is no other protection against bad stuff.

Psychological Problems

Younger men may have two difficulties with dope that most older men will not experience. First, young people commonly believe themselves to be immortal and indestructible. Nothing really bad has happened to them, so nothing will, they think. This attitude passes with time and experience, but in drug use it has to be guarded against lest it cause a lot of trouble.

Second, the younger a man is, the stronger a certain temptation: on leaving childhood he faces a new life with new demands and difficulties, just as he does when entering gay life. When he is growing up and accepting himself as homosexual at the same time, the learning process can be all the more unpleasant. It's easy to smooth the way by dropping a pill or smoking a joint. But if a man lets drugs take care of the rough spots, then he avoids learning to deal with them himself. Obviously, this is a mistake. In extreme cases a man will remain a child mentally, with a needle or capsule substituting for Mommy.

Among older men, those who are perhaps a little self-conscious about performance in bed may try one thing or another for a sexually stimulating effect. Some drugs do enhance sensuality, as has been pointed out; however, there is no true aphrodisiac except for a few substances that unfortunately also happen to be deadly poisons. And the dope that might improve matters sexually can also make a man more nervous, rather than less.

The important thing about drugs is that there is no free lunch. Maybe this sounds like pious moralizing, but it's physiology. Some drugs, such as marijuana, give a good deal more, so far as is known, than they ask in return. Others can be used occasionally with little harm, and still others are exceedingly dangerous, physically and mentally. Most substances discussed here will eventually create either physical addiction or psychological dependence. Also, generally speaking, extended exposure to a drug habituates you to it; that is, the more you take, the more you need in order to achieve the same level of high. Here's where the no-free-lunch rule comes down the hardest: generally a drug's entertainment value lessens considerably as dependence takes hold.

If dope is to be part of your life, you must remain strong and keep its influence weak, no more than a pleasant diversion. Drugs will not solve your life's problems.

15 The Police

Oh, oh, I thought — caught in the act — in *fragrant delicious.*
— Phil Andros

For anyone who is gay and sexually active, the folk wisdom about an ounce of prevention being worth a pound of cure applies full force. It may be unsettling to think about problems with the law, but to ignore them risks an inconvenience and a drain on your finances, at the very least. At the worst you could be sent to prison or killed.

Criminal law as it applies to gay men is a complicated matter, and has become more so with changes in recent years. Laws vary greatly depending where you live. In many places, any sexual contact between persons of the same sex is illegal under any circumstances. Anal intercourse (known legally as sodomy or, quaintly, as the infamous crime against nature) and cocksucking (AKA fellatio or oral copulation or, sometimes, sodomy) often are punishable by a term in state prison.

Until a few years ago this was the law almost everywhere in the United States. Lately a number of states have significantly liberalized their laws, so that cocksucking and anal sex are legal if they take place between consenting adults in private. And the harsher laws in some states have been struck down by court decisions. Attempts have been made to get a ruling from the Supreme Court, but so far without success.

Many complexities arise because, whatever a state's laws may be, enforcement can vary drastically, not only from one time to another, but also from one place to another. In the days when the laws on same-sex conduct in California were among the toughest in the country, gays were not bothered terribly much in San Francisco, but in Los Angeles they were searched out and prosecuted with zeal.

Even where it's legal for consenting male adults to have sex with each other in private, the situation is still not simple. What does "in private" mean? Legally speaking, is a three-way or a four-way or an all-out orgy private? How about sex in a cubicle in a gay bath? (We wouldn't bet on it.) From your bedroom with the curtains drawn to the bushes of a city park, the extremes of private and public sex frame an almost infinite range of undecided legal possibilities.

Further, however liberal the laws, you can't assume that *all* your sexual activities are legal. In general, the courts hold that nobody can consent to any activity which leads to his or her injury. And this raises a question: can sex which causes physical harm, even a little (bruises, welts, etc.), be reason for prosecution? However willingly you may engage in S&M practices, a good many of them could be illegal.

Certain acts are still against the law everywhere. One of them is sex in public. A bar, gay or not, is considered a public place; it is not at all certain that its status is altered when it charges a membership fee and calls itself a private club.

A public toilet is always a public place, no matter how remote its location or slight its use. (A lawyer of our acquaintance argued in court that the men's restroom in which his client was arrested was not a public place because approximately half the public was excluded from it; the judge admired the argument but did not buy it.)

Another act that is still against the law almost everywhere is to solicit another person to engage in a sex act. Whether payment is involved or not doesn't matter, nor whether the contemplated action is to take place in private or not.

Next, the laws that protect consenting adults from prosecution do not apply when anyone underage is in the

144 COMING OUT RIGHT

picture. Relations are criminal not only between an adult and a minor but also between two minors, and the crime is judged greater or lesser for the adult according to the age of the minor involved. For example, we know of a case where two adult men had sex with two brothers, age thirteen and fourteen. The guy who made it with the younger brother went to prison, but the other remained free. The testimony of the thirteen-year-old did not by that state's law have to be coroborated by any other evidence. However, the testimony of his brother, only one year older, did require some further proof, and there wasn't any.

Finally, in certain occupations, a brush with the law over sexual conduct can have much graver consequences. For instance, the relatively liberal California court upheld the revoking of a school teacher's certificate because she had been observed in a private group-sex scene going down on a man.

Opportunities for arrest

If you are gay, there are three main avenues to the jug. The first is to be caught in *flagrante delicto*; that is, to be discovered in the act of doing something illegal, such as having sex in public. (It's the same whether the cops happen upon you, or if they spy on the action by secret surveillance.)

The second route is commonly called entrapment. This means the police set you up by using undercover operatives.

Entrapment is illegal, so if you can prove that it was used in arranging your arrest, the charge against you has to be thrown out. However, this is not easy to do. For one thing, in situations that involve sexual offenses the courts rarely go along with entrapment claims. For another, the *legal* definition of entrapment is far more narrow than many people realize.

For example, California has one of the most liberal definitions: entrapment is said to occur when the conduct of law enforcement officers is such that it would induce a normally law-abiding person to commit an offense. Sounds great for the defendant, but consider: how many (presumably heterosexual) judges would ever take the position that a "normally law-abiding person" would under any circumstances whatsoever play with someone else's cock in a public toilet?

Right.

In addition, on a practical level, an undercover police officer usually can get away with anything short of making the first overt physical move. He leaves that to you, and when you make that first move, you've had it. (Typical police testimony: "Then he reached for my private parts. . . .")

The third and most difficult way to get free room and board from the taxpayer is via the raid. Men who are beginning to explore a gay lifestyle commonly have great fears of being picked up in a police raid.

Well, bars and baths and porno movies and such *do* get raided; still, though the pattern varies a great deal, the chances that you will ever find yourself in a raid are pretty slight. (We are assuming that you will only patronize legitimate operations and will stay away from dives that are knee-deep in drug dealing and folks who want to sell you a stereo they just happen to have out in the car, and that you will not make a habit of sucking off bartenders during their working hours.)

In steam bath raids all the patrons may be taken to the station and charged with the crime of being present in a disorderly house. This is a minor charge and will rarely stick.

If you happen to be present in a gay bar when it is raided, you are not likely to get arrested; and if you are, you probably won't be charged; and if you are, it's doubtful that you will have to stand trial.

If this sounds rather strange to you, it's because police raids on bars and other gay establishments are not exactly what they appear to be. Sometimes they are intended to look like moral crusades. That is, the raid is a public relations device engineered by public officials and police administrators to demonstrate to the public that they are not soft on pervert sin. Such raids frequently occur just before local elections.

Otherwise the purpose of the police raid is to harass the

gay establishment, and this may stem from either of two motives. There may be pressure to put the bar out of business (and nothing will ruin a bar's patronage faster than word spreading that it is the target of raids). Or, in locales where payoffs are still a recognized substitute for licensing of gay establishments, the raid is a way of suggesting to the owner that he begin, or increase, such payoffs.

Therefore, as a customer you are merely a pawn of little importance to the raid's real goal. If you do get arrested, you may simply be taken to the station, detained for a while, then released without charge. Or you may be charged under some vague statute which eventually will be dismissed. After all, the public remembers only the headlines announcing the arrests, and rarely learns about the ultimate outcome of those arrested.

If publicity is often the primary purpose of a raid, that is also the major threat to any gay man who is highly closeted. It is increasingly less common, but in some cities the local newspaper will still print the names of persons arrested in a raid, and police have been known to inform relatives or employers. This latter practice has been curbed somewhat from fear of lawsuits. However, keeping up with the electronic revolution, the cops have sometimes arrived accompanied by television crews.

How not to get arrested
The basic rule to follow is to be familiar with the applicable laws in your part of the world and, whether they are liberal or prehistoric, the extent to which they are enforced. Knowing this, you can act accordingly.

If you're not sure what's what, be guided by the following:
1. Don't ask anyone home for sex; invite him for a drink or to look at your etchings or anything else.
2. If you like high-risk sex in public settings, or there is a high probability that you might hit on an undercover agent, remember to stay sober and undrugged, to let the other guy make the first move whenever possible, and try to develop a sixth sense for people; bad vibes mean *clear out at once*.

3. If your favorite brand of sex is wild, far-out, or just plain bizarre, be discreet about it in proportion to its weirdness. Discretion is also important when anyone underage is involved in sexual activity.
4. In bars, keep your hands and other body parts to yourself.
5. When traveling, never assume that the laws where you're headed are the same as at home. Even if they are, enforcement could be far different.

If you do get arrested

Basically, stay cool. Try to keep your wits about you, and tell the police no more than is absolutely necessary. In any case *do none of the following* at the moment of arrest: hassle the officer in any way; interfere in the arrest of anyone else (you can do him a lot more good on the outside than if you are next to him in a cell); beg for favors from the cops (a plea such as "Please don't let my wife find out about this!" will probably hurt more than help); talk the officer out of making the arrest or explain away your conduct — most likely you'll say something that can be used against you.

As the arrest process continues, remember five points:

First, you are obliged to identify yourself to the police. This means telling them your name and home address; showing your I.D. should be sufficient. Never give an alias or a phoney address. At some point you will have to give information such as your date of birth so they can check for any previous police record, but this may not occur until you reach the station. There, when you are booked, you will be fingerprinted. At no time do you have to tell the police the identity of your employer or who the members of your family are.

Second, don't talk. Say nothing about the events which led to your arrest. When you are questioned about the bust, say politely but firmly, "I want to talk to a lawyer before I discuss this." Repeat this as often as necessary, no matter how sick you get of saying it, until they cease their questioning. And speak up: the more people who hear you say this, the better. Under no circumstances should you give the police any kind of written or recorded statement.

Third, don't resist searches, but do protest them. Make no physical resistance whatsoever if the police pat down your clothing or search your pockets. But do tell them that you are not consenting to this. This should always be done, but is especially important if you have anything to hide, like a joint in your shirt pocket. The same goes if the police want to search your car or even your apartment or house. State clearly and as often as discretion permits that you do not consent to the search and that you have surrendered the key (or unlocked the door) only because the police have ordered you to do so. Whether the search is legal is something to be fought out in court; arguing this point with the cops is useless.

Fourth, do your best, where possible, to get out of jail before making any decision about pleading innocent or guilty to anything. Most people find jail a frightening and depressing experience, and for gays it can be especially grim. The temptation is strong to get it over with as quickly as possible on whatever terms you're offered. But remember, you can't expect the police to give you objective advice, and anything you're told by other jail inmates will probably be grossly inaccurate. You will have an entirely different perspective once you are back in the familiar world outside.

These days there is a trend toward releasing persons who do not have serious records and who are not charged with violent crimes on their own recognizance (often called "O.R."). This avoids the expense of bail, but you may have to remain in custody longer while your eligibility for O.R. is checked out. In that process your employment may have to be verified, which a highly closeted man would find unacceptable.

Ask what you have to do to get O.R.'d at the time you're booked. Practice varies. In some places, particularly larger cities, court functionaries routinely interview inmates for such release. Elsewhere you'll have to wait until you are taken before the judge for arraignment, then ask him to O.R. you. Court does not meet on weekends.

Bail is the alternative to O.R. Assuming you have or can get the money, it will get you out of the slammer quickly, even on a weekend or holiday. You will be allowed to make at least one completed telephone call after you have been booked. Don't waste it. Contact somebody who is dependable, who will do what has to be done to get you out. If you are in a strange city or without funds, you may have to use a bail bondsman. His charges run about ten percent of the amount of your bail.

You may not be able to get out of jail at all if you have been ignoring such small legal matters as parking tickets. Any warrant issued on a citation can spoil your chances for release.

If you have no choice but to remain in jail, request to be placed in the queen's tank or otherwise segregated from heterosexual inmates. *Do this at the time of booking.* This is especially important if your sexual orientation is obvious, or if the charge against you makes it evident. In most instances the authorities will comply with your request. It isn't that they want to do you any favors; they merely know they can be sued if you should be raped or otherwise brutalized.

Fifth, no matter how hopeless you consider your case to be, get a lawyer, one who is familiar with the local criminal courts. Ultimately you may have to plead guilty to something, but what offense you admit to can make a huge difference in your life. Your lawyer may be able to negotiate an agreement with the prosecutor to let you plead guilty to something less serious. It might even be possible to plead to a charge which has no obvious sexual overtones, such as disturbing the peace. This can make the difference in whether you have to register as a sex offender, whether your employment or professional license is jeopardized, and whether you would be considered a repeat offender should you be arrested again in the future. If your line of work requires you to be bonded, the conviction will have to be disclosed on every job application you fill out. Finally, your lawyer may be able to save you from having to agree, as a condition of probation, to submit to some demeaning program of "therapy" that's designed to force you into a heterosexual behavior pattern.

Briefly, these are the things to remember:
1. Tell the police politely *only* what they have a right to know.
2. Make no statements about the cause of your arrest.
3. Neither resist searches nor consent to them.
4. Do your best to get out of jail.
5. Get a lawyer.

Arrest and the underage gay man. Most of the above does not apply to anyone who is underage. In juvenile court, typically there is no right to bail and only limited rights concerning privacy and the giving of statements.

Crimes against gay men

Merely by being homosexual we are peculiarly the targets of two very different kinds of criminal activities. The first and more common is mugging or fag-bashing.

Attacks by homophobes are all too common; they range from verbal harassment to bottles thrown from passing cars to beatings with fists or attacks with clubs, knives, or pistols. Grave injury and sometimes death can result.

Fag-bashers are almost always male teenagers or young adults. They attack in groups, not alone. They can be members of some inner-city minority or they can be "nice" middle-class white kids from suburbia.

Muggings of gay men tend to be more common at night, of course, in the areas they frequent or on their ill-lit outskirts. Sometimes cars parked near gay establishments are vandalized.

The first and best protection is to keep alert while you are out in the street, especially near gay bars or in gay neighborhoods. It helps to avoid being obviously drunk or wrecked, to know the local turf, and to stay out of bad-news areas whenever possible.

Many gays maintain a low profile in public, and while this is not acceptable to some, it is nevertheless a useful means of self-protection. Campy as some men carry on in the bars, they change their manner the moment they're outside. Others, when their clothing makes their sexual orientation obvious, will wear a long coat out in the streets.

If you are attacked you may be alone, outnumbered, surprised, and weaponless. Even so, you still may be able to save your skin or at least lessen the damage. First, make a lot of noise. Scream as loud as you can. Nobody may come to your aid, and no one may call the police, but either out of morbid curiosity or a genuine desire to help you, people in the area will often turn on house and porch lights. This, or merely the uproar you're making, may convince the bashers to split.

If they have come by car, another way to get them to go away in a hurry is to yell out the automobile's license number over and over again. Remember, cars can easily be traced to their owners. With adolescents the car is probably in Dad's name, and junior does not want to get into hot water with the old man. (In any case, if a car is involved, get the license number.)

In some urban areas civilian patrols of gay men keep an eye out for exactly this sort of trouble. Where these groups have formed, gays are encouraged to carry very loud whistles. Like yelling, its use in summoning aid may by itself scare off the bashers.

You might choose to carry Mace, but in many cities you must have a license from the police to do so. Like any weapon it has limits and can be taken away and used against you.

Tempting as it may be to have a gun or knife with you, using either is likely to lead to a jail sentence, and carrying a concealed weapon generally is a crime in itself. Besides, knife-fighting is an art that has to be learned and practiced.

It is not a bad idea to study some kind of self-defense. However, you have to keep it up, and you can do so by making it part of your exercise program. The karate you learned five years ago and haven't tried since will be too rusty to be much help when you suddenly need to defend yourself.

If you have none of these means of protection when you are attacked, there are other measures you can take First, as a matter of safety, take off your glasses if you can see well without them.

If you are encircled, being backed down an alley or against a wall, pick out the least impressive member of the gang as its weakest point, and charge through the line there. Do it as fast, hard, and suddenly as you can. Surprise is everything. Then run like hell.

If you choose to fight, or if the choice is made for you, consider that being outnumbered gives you the right to get plenty dirty to protect yourself. The great problem here is that most civilized people must overcome a strong reluctance to commit physical brutalities. Get over it as fast as you can. Look around for weapons — a piece of board, a bottle, preferably broken, a tin can lid, a brick or a rock. A ring of keys, if held in your fist, can add a lot to your punch. And don't forget the more vulnerable parts of the human anatomy. Even if you're down and getting punched or kicked, try while protecting yourself to punch or kick back as hard as you can.

Again, whatever else you do, make as much noise as possible: scream bloody murder.

If you plead or whine you are likely to be beaten up much worse than if you fight back. This is psychology, not heroics. Win, lose, or draw, if you defend yourself you'll feel better in the morning.

The second crime to which gay men are exposed is blackmail. Extortion, as it is called in the law, probably was far more common in the pre-liberation days than it is now. One of the strongest arguments for coming out of the closet is that it makes blackmail impossible — unless you let yourself be photographed committing an illegal act. And blackmail remains a serious problem for men who become sexually involved with preadolescent boys.

It is doubtful that you will ever find yourself the subject of a blackmail attempt, but if it happens there is a single ironclad rule to follow: *Never, under any circumstances, give in to the blackmailer's demands.*

Sure, he'll guarantee that as soon as you give him the money he's leaving forever to begin a new life in Brazil or

Finland. But inevitably you'll hear from him again the next time he's hard-up for cash.

Anyone who will stoop to blackmail does not think twice about passing off a copy of the incriminating matter as the original. Bear in mind that photographic negatives can be duplicated and that it's easy to make very good photocopies of documents and letters.

Call the blackmailer's bluff and you destroy his power over you. If he persists, tell him you intend to go to the police. If necessary, *you must be prepared to do this.* Of course, if the blackmailer is threatening physical harm and is likely to carry out the threat, then go straight to the authorities without confronting him.

Getting involved with the cops, much as you dread the thought, is made easier by the likelihood that however much the average police inspector may hate homosexuals, he probably loathes extortionists even more.

Don't go to a patrolman or to the local precinct station. Contact the criminal investigation section at headquarters. If you get the run-around, see a lawyer. In fact, you might want to do that first thing, especially if the subject of the blackmail attempt is something such as sex with a boy which could get you into serious trouble if exposed.

The police may want you to set up the blackmailer by pretending to go along with his demands. If you won't do this, it may be impossible to prove that he is an extortionist. Remember, the more proof the police can gather, the smaller the chance of a trial at which you will have to testify. If you must appear as a witness, be sure you tell the truth under oath, no matter how unsavory.

The best practical protection against blackmail is to generate no physical evidence that could be used against you. In a his-word-against-yours situation a blackmailer can rarely get anywhere. Therefore, the more closeted you feel you must remain, the greater care you should take about such things as letters, diaries, photographs, and checks.

Calling the police

Here is another area in which gay people face widespread discrimination, because in many communities the police are openly and unashamedly homophobic.

This largely accounts for their notorious indifference in responding to bashings or disturbances outside gay bars. The police rationalize their inaction on the ground that it's not worth the bother since a jury, getting wind of the true nature of the event, would not convict anyhow. This is especially a reason for failure to prosecute when a gay man has been ripped off or assaulted by someone he's picked up for sex.

If the law enforcement people in your locality are definitely unsympathetic to gays, it will be of little use to report minor skirmishes or near-misses with fag-bashers to them. Even if you get creamed, the cop's sympathy easily may be with your assailants. *They*, after all, are normal, red-blooded guys, to a cop's mind, so he may feel it is *you* who constitutes the problem. Besides, as a teenager he may have punched out a few homosexuals himself. A cop with this attitude, should he find illicit drugs on you, say, or a phoney I.D., might well take you down to the station and let your attackers go free.

However the police view the incident, if there is a gay patrol group in your area, report any major or minor street hassles to it at once. Your information may be a great help. Where the authorities are not interested, be sure the patrol gets any evidence you have — physical descriptions, license numbers, any wallet or other source of identification that may have fallen in battle. With sufficient evidence the organization may be able to pressure the cops into taking some useful action.

If you are badly beaten and end up in the emergency room of a hospital, the police will probably take notice as a matter of course.

Where you do report a fag-bashing to the authorities, be sure to make two things clear: first, that you were sober, or nearly so, at the time of the attack. Second, emphasize that you did not make a pass at any of the assailants.

This is important because bashers commonly defend their actions by saying something like "We were minding our own business when this queer came on with me, so I got angry, and . . . ." Alas, a very few muggings *are* prompted in this way, by some messed-up or just plain dizzy queen who goes indiscriminately flirting and teasing up and down the streets.

If the crime against you is clearly related to your sexual orientation (bashing, rape, robbery by a sex partner, etc.), your only course is to be direct. The police interview can be almost as disagreeable as the crime itself. You might find it easier to have someone with you at the time, a lawyer if you have one, your therapist, or at least a friend. It's a situation where moral support can be extremely comforting.

Where the gay element in a crime is not obvious or non-existent, as when your apartment is burgled while you are away, the police are more likely to be polite and helpful. Like many other straight men, cops can live with the knowledge that you are gay as long as they don't have to deal with it openly. So, if gay is irrelevant, you don't need to make a point of bringing it up. You might even consider toning it down, by removing that painting of the very nude male from over the fireplace or covering the pile of skin mags with a copy of *Farm Journal*. True, this hardly adds to a sense of gay pride or counts as yet another victory for the principles of the Bill of Rights. But a good argument can be made for the value of tact, diplomacy, and manipulation.

Problematic as police protection may be for gay people, do not *assume* that you won't get it. The situation differs from place to place, and in some large cities law officers calmly deal with gay men and women as they do with any others. This is not yet common, and it doesn't just happen. Usually it is publicity and political pressure that helps gays obtain the same consideration and protection as other citizens. In San Francisco, for instance, the police department recruits gay people and has a gay liaison committee.

Hairy as all of this may sound to you, the fact is that the vast majority of gay men have never been accused of a crime, have never consulted a criminal lawyer, have never seen the inside of a jail or been summoned to a courtroom, have never been blackmailed, and have almost never been fag-bashed. You do not need to worry as long as you exercise reasonable care in regard to matters of crime and law enforcement.

16 Friends, Roommates, Lovers

> Patience! Patience! The world is a vast and ghastly intricacy of mechanism and one has to be very wary, not to get mangled in it.
>
> — D. H. Lawrence

Gay people relate to each other socially in ways that often have no exact counterpart in the straight world. Friendship assumes a much greater importance among gays than among heterosexuals. Friends may replace the lost links with the family, and they help you contact other gays in a subculture that is for the most part invisible in the greater society. Their importance does not end with social and sexual life. Because of discrimination that gay people face in such things as employment, bank loans, and housing, we often have little choice but to turn to friends for support and assistance.

For straights a roommate of the same sex is common during college years or when starting out in the world, but is soon replaced with marriage. Many gay people, however, expect to live with one or more roommates throughout their lives.

The roommate may or may not be a lover. Since legally there is no such thing as marriage between two persons of the same sex, gays must be satisfied with living together.

This arrangement has a long history among homosexuals, though it has become more or less acceptable only recently for straights.

Those laws which define certain sexual activities as criminal are the only ones that apply as such to gay relationships. Many gay people therefore assume that aside from this they live in a legal vacuum. This is not so. The rules by which heterosexual society regulates its relationships also apply to the gay world, with results that are sometimes absurd and on occasion can be tragic.

Consider some fairly common situations:

Kevin has a new lover, Bruce, who wants to buy a sports car. But Bruce can't qualify for a loan by himself. The bank will lend the money only if Kevin co-signs a four-year promissory note. He does. Six months later their beautiful relationship has gone sour, and it ends abruptly when Bruce drives off to points unknown. The bank expects Kevin to take over the payments, but he is naturally rather angry about the situation and refuses to do so. The bank garnishes his paycheck. Kevin's boss tells him he'll be terminated if he doesn't get the garnishment removed.

That's one. Here's another:

Getting the bank off his back somehow, Kevin vows that he is through with lovers forever. Even so, he doesn't want to live in a dinky studio. His friend Bob, he feels, would make a compatible roommate. Together they locate a beautiful apartment whose spacious living room has French windows that give a splendid view of the park. The only problem is they're not curtained. The roommates decide to go halves, with Bob paying Kevin off bit by bit and Kevin arranging time payments with the Bon Ton Department Store, which sends out two charming guys to install some lovely custom drapes.

A few months later Kevin meets Charles, and it's mad love. They want to live together, so Kevin takes up residence in Charles' condominium. Bob, stuck with double his usual rent until he can locate another roommate or a smaller abode, can't afford to take over the payments for the draperies and declines to do so. The curtains, being custom made, are useless for any other location, so the Bon Ton leans on Kevin, warning him that he'll be taken to court if he doesn't cough up.

Now consider this one:

Kevin and Charles have been living together in the condo, and very happily, for a number of years. (Something has to work out right for Kevin, you say? Well. . . .) All this time they have deposited their paychecks in a single joint checking account, and from it they have made payments on the condominium (though they haven't taken it out of Charles' name), purchased household furniture including a number of valuable antiques, and paid their other bills.

One terrible day Charles suffers a disabling stroke which requires that he be cared for in a nursing home. His family, which has never accepted his gay lifestyle or his lover, has a court appoint Charles' brother Snotley as conservator of the property. Operating under a perfectly legal court order, Snot puts the condo up for sale, grabs the antiques, ties up the bank account, and gives Kevin notice to vacate the premises.

None of these illustrations is far-fetched. Each represents a kind of predicament that countless gay men have gotten themselves into. These problems are not inevitable, however, and can be avoided by always sticking close to two basic rules when dealing with friends, roommates, and lovers.

First, don't enter into any kind of financial commitment that is based merely on the continued existence of a relationship, unless you are monumentally assured that the relationship indeed will continue. This is especially important early on, when you should *never* co-sign a note or lend a substantial sum of money. (And if a lover ever asks you to prove your devotion with your checkbook, get suspicious fast.) If and when you relax this principle, preferably after years, not months, remain aware that there is still a potential for problems. This is pointedly necessary in any long-term investment situation. (Many a beautiful home has ended up for sale by judge's order as ex-lovers glare at each other across the courtroom.)

Second, know the legal and monetary effects of your actions, and take the necessary steps to protect yourself.

To this end, it may be wise to consider some of the basics that are involved in sharing your life with others.

Renting together

Whether it's love or convenience, when you share a place with another person you inescapably involve yourself with two other people — your roommate and the landlord.

First, you and your prospective roommate or lover should decide exactly what each of you is to contribute in terms of rent, utilities, groceries, furnishings, and household chores. If you two are strictly roommates, you should also discuss social ground rules about such matters as pets, smoking, parties, and tricks. You may discover in this process that you shouldn't share a rental after all, which is too bad but better than finding out later.

Assuming you have worked out matters, write up a simple agreement about the basics. This can include not only the amount of rent each will pay and such as that, but also the disposition of the apartment should you two want to discontinue being roommates.

This agreement is binding between yourselves, but remember that it is not binding on your landlord. When you have it worked out between you, then you arrange the rental with him. The simplest route is to rent the place jointly. That way, you are both tenants as far as he is concerned, and he can look to either of you for payment of the entire rent. However, landlords often won't accept this form of rental because it makes evictions, always a hassle, even more difficult.

The other way is for one of the couple to rent the place, then sublet to the other. The fact that two people will be living there must be made clear to the landlord, however, and be agreeable to him or her. Otherwise, the landlord has sure grounds for terminating the rental.

When more than two people want to rent a place, a big old house, say, the landlord is almost sure to insist on a single legal tenant.

Whether it's a joint or single tenancy, there are two basic

types of rental arrangements for residential real estate. The **informal rental agreement** runs for a relatively short period of time, usually but not always thirty days, and ordinarily it's called a month-to-month agreement. This arrangement need not be set out in writing, though it is not uncommon for the landlord to require that the tenant sign a written rental agreement or a statement of conditions of tenancy or some similar document.

Either renter or landlord can terminate this type of rental by giving notice equal to the period of tenancy; that is, if it's a month-to-month rental, thirty day's notice is required. This arrangement makes it easy to leave the place if it or the roommate proves unsuitable, or if you want to move on.

However, it has several disadvantages. Unless there is some sort of rent control in your locality, you are helpless against any increases the landlord may choose to impose. And you can be tossed out any time, as long as the landlord gives you proper notice. In recent years some local and state governments have passed laws that limit arbitrary rental terminations, but in general the owner of the property can put you out in the street for any reason whatsoever.

A good protection against these hazards is the **lease**, which is the other basic type of rental agreement. On residential property the lease usually runs for one year, but it can be written for a longer time if agreeable to lessor and lessee.

A lease must be in writing. No alterations can be made in it except in writing. A lease is also a good deal more than an agreement: it is a formal contract. This means you are going to have a problem getting out of it if your roommate turns out to be a lemon, or if for any reason you wish to leave the rental before the year is up.

Of course you should read the lease carefully and be sure you understand everything before you sign it. The form leases commonly used by landlords were not drawn up with the tenants' interests as the primary concern, and their legalese is not always easy to understand. When this is the case, get someone besides the landlord or rental agent to explain it to you. Whether this proves necessary or not, you should look out for two provisions in particular.

First, the lease may state that the premises may not be sublet without the landlord's permission. Make certain that an addition is made to the effect that the landlord consents to your subletting to one or however many roommates you plan to have.

The second provision to watch out for is the one that says the rental unit cannot be shared by persons who are not related to each other. Obviously, it has to be taken out.

Whatever is added to or subtracted from the lease, be sure it is done *before* you sign it.

A joint lease, where two or more people sign, is not unknown, but it has one huge disadvantage that should make you very cautious: a breach of the lease by any one signer can be considered a breach on the part of all. In short, you could be thrown out because of a roommate's wild parties, even if they take place on weekends when you're out of town. It's generally a better idea, especially with more than two roommates, for one to sign the lease and for the others to sublet from him.

Moving into someone else's place

If there's no lease, simply ask the landlord if he consents to a second tenant in the rental unit. If he does, he's likely to raise the rent somewhat, and it may be necessary to sign a new agreement, one that fits the altered situation.

If there is a lease prohibiting sublets or double occupancy, you'll have to get the landlord's permission in writing. Sometimes, especially with an absentee owner, tenants figure that nobody will notice if a friend moves in with them. Well, many landlords keep a closer watch on their property than their tenants may realize. If they find that a renter is breaching his agreement or contract, they have a perfectly legal reason for throwing him and his friend out.

Some things to remember

First, whoever signs the rental agreement or the lease is responsible for the rent. Again, squabbles about this can be minimized when tenants who share have a written agreement with each other.

Second, if your roommate can't come up with the rent in time, or runs up a phone bill he can't pay, be sure you get some kind of I.O.U. from him in writing if you cover his share. Then, should he refuse to pay later or skip out, written evidence will make it easier to get a judgment against him in small claims court. (Of course if the ex-roommate has no job or assets, it may still be impossible to collect the money.)

Third, if the signer of the agreement or lease leaves the rental unit, the other tenants have no legal right to keep the place. They will have to arrange a new agreement with the landlord, assuming he wants them to stay.

Fourth, in the case where roommates each want the other to leave, it's the signer of the lease or agreement who has the right to stay.

Fifth, an ugly reality: in all but a handful of communities which have enacted laws banning discrimination against gays, the landlord can rent or not as he or she pleases. Therefore, the gay man as prospective or actual tenant can run into several different situations. Some property owners refuse to rent to two or more men, regarding all such arrangements as suspicious. Some won't rent to men they believe are gay or, fearing the noise of parties and late hours, will not rent to young men. Others will try to evict men whom they discover to be gay.

There is a positive side to this depressing coin. In these days of limited rental housing in many cities and of rising prices, all kinds of people are living in roommate or communal situations which therefore do not appear so questionable as they once did. And many landlords don't give a damn about anything but the rent and the condition of the property. There are gay landlords, gay apartment buildings, and gay neighborhoods.

Finally, a fair number of landlords (whether or not homosexual themselves) prefer gay male tenants, especially those renters who are older or settled in their lives. Because gay men don't want to draw undue notice from owners or other tenants, they tend to be quiet, discreet about their lives, and to mind their own business. Among other things this means they pay the rent promptly and do their own minor repairs instead of calling the apartment manager or realty office every time a faucet leaks.

An elderly, straight and rather naive apartment building owner once explained to us his crafty way of identifying gay men among prospective tenants: "I show 'em the place, and if they want to paint the bathroom, then I know they are, so I rent to 'em."

The problems of shared housing can be avoided entirely, by the way, if each of two lovers has his own place to live. During the work week they are out of each other's hair, which minimizes strains in the relationship, and from Friday to Monday one of them "vacations" at the other's place. This may or may not work as a long-term arrangement, but it's worth considering at the beginning of a serious relationship, before you are sure just how far it may develop.

Sharing things

Where there is an equal contribution by each person in such goods as household furnishings, then the rights of both people are relatively easy to define. However, some other situations can become almost unbelievably complicated. Lovers especially can unknowingly drift into a tangle of financial and legal relationships. It all may begin with the joint purchase of a waterbed and go on eventually to buying a home.

Suppose Robert and Jim, who are devoted to each other, decide to fix up an old house. Robert can't hammer a nail straight, but he has a full-time job and makes good money. Jim is a skilled carpenter with time on his hands during the slow season. So Robert puts up most of the cash, and Jim does most of the work. Obviously the potential for difficulties is great. Before they start work on the place, Jim and Robert should carefully discuss and set down the details of the understanding between them.

Even a simple written agreement can be legally enforceable, and this is much to the advantage of gay people. The law is tailored to the needs of straight society alone; it does not recognize the existence of gay relationships. Partners in a hetero marriage will have their rights defined for them by the courts if they don't do this for themselves. But a homosexual couple, however long-lasting and devoted their relationship, or short-term and stormy, only has rights in terms of agreements, partnerships, contracts and such.

Written agreements. Whether you draw up an agreement yourselves or have it prepared by a lawyer should be determined by the complexity of the circumstances. But every agreement, even the simplest, should cover certain matters:
1. The respective obligation of each party to contribute and the respective share of each party's ownership.
2. Disposition of the property if the couple splits up or for some other reason can no longer continue to share. If the property can be easily divided, then no problem; but if items are not identical, you must be specific about who gets what. If one party is to have the right to buy the other's interest, the agreement will have to indicate two things: how it will be determined who has the right to buy the other out and the method of determining the value of the property.
3. Disposition of the property if one of the parties should die. There's one thing your agreement *cannot* do: transfer the dead partner's share of the property to the survivor. (Only a will can do this.) The agreement can provide that the survivor has the right to purchase the deceased's share from his estate, and can specify, again, the way the value of the share is to be arrived at.

A simple agreement does not have to be set up in any particular form or use legal phrases. It does have to be unambiguous and understandable. It also, in order to enforced by the courts, cannot be manifestly unfair, nor can it be a transparent attempt to evade making out a will. For instance, it would be no use to give the survivor the right to buy the dead partner's interest for some nominal sum such as one dollar. Your sexual relationship should not be mentioned in any way, lest the agreement be declared void as against public policy. The agreement should be dated and signed by all parties. Photocopies and carbon copies are valid, but each one should be signed individually.

Here is an example of an agreement that two men living together could draw up for themselves. It is meant only as an illustration and *not* as an ideal form; note that it covers the situations the two guys are likely to encounter and that it deals with each of the three points made above.

AGREEMENT

George Smith and Richard Jones agree that the household furnishings they intend to purchase together will be their shared property with each of them having a one-half interest in this property. They agree that each of them will be responsible for paying half of the cost of these furnishings. If either of them has not paid his full share of the cost, the unpaid balance of his share will be a debt owed to the other party.

If the parties should no longer be sharing living quarters, the party remaining in the living quarters shall have the right to buy the other's interest. If neither of them remains in their former shared quarters, and they are unable to agree on some other disposition of their furnishings, the parties will take turns choosing items in such a manner that they each end up with property of approximately equal value. If the parties cannot agree on the value of the property, it will be appraised by a competent appraiser of their joint selection. If they are unable to agree on an appraiser, they will each select an appraiser, and the value of each item of property will be the average of the two appraisals.

If one of the parties should die, the survivor shall have the right to buy the decedent's interest. If there is a dispute as to the value of the property, it shall be determined by a competent appraiser of the survivor's selection.

Dated: _____, 19____   (signed) George Smith
                                  (signed) Richard Jones

Agreements made by lawyers. Where your involvement with a partner goes beyond such simple matters as the mutual ownership of household goods, you should probably not try to draft anything yourselves but rather should have an agreement drawn up by a lawyer. The labyrinths of complication that Robert and Jim can get into with the house they are fixing up definitely call for the services of an attorney. Otherwise they may find it extremely difficult to satisfactorily place a value on Jim's non-monetary contribution, and since real property is involved they must be sure that all legal formalities affecting its title are strictly complied with.

Men who go into business together certainly need a lawyer (and an accountant as well). Any man who once was married and has children to support will need help to make the sometimes elaborate legal moves necessary to insulate himself and his partner from claims the family can make on him.

Many people believe that only the rich go to lawyers. Straights may be able to get through life with this attitude, since the laws are made for them, but the majority of gays sooner or later will benefit from sound legal advice from a competent professional. (Finding a lawyer is discussed in Chapter 18.)

Changes ahead? — The Marvin case

Everyone interested in the basically nonexistent legal status of gay relationships is closely watching a recent development in the law, nicknamed palimony. The live-in lady friend of actor Lee Marvin brought suit against him after the end of their relationship, claiming she was entitled to a share of his property just as though she had been his lawful wife. She felt she deserved this because she had agreed to give up her own career as part of the understanding they had reached with each other.

The court ruled that if she could prove that she and Marvin had in fact made such an agreement, then she could recover under it. Nothing was said to indicate that this ruling was limited to situations involving persons of opposite sex. Therefore, some lawyers feel that the Marvin decision opens the way for legally-sanctioned same-sex relationships based on agreements between the parties.

Well, possibly, but two things should be kept in mind. First, the Marvin decision was made in a California court and applies only in that state. To some extent the ruling reflects a peculiarity of California law: unlike most states it does not recognize common-law marriage. (And so far there has been no stampede by other states to follow the California court's example.)

Second, the ruling is so new that we do not yet know exactly what application it will have to gay relationships, even in the Golden State. It does suggest, though, that any well-to-do gay male citizen of California who takes on the support of a lover should think seriously about a written agreement, one that clearly defines the relationship of the lover to the wealthier man's earnings and property.

A final caution

Written agreements can make breakups a lot easier to manage, but all the complicated partnership arrangements and legal papers in the world cannot save a bad relationship. There is no use trying to be roommates with someone you honestly don't like. Teaming up with a friend in business is a very poor way of getting him to be your lover. Sometimes, when a gay relationship gets shaky, the pair plunge into some apparently cementing situation such as buying a home or going into business together. (In the straight world the equivalent is having a baby to save the marriage.) Most men end up discovering that problems are not solved by getting deeper into complications.

17 Looking Ahead

> The entire system of man's affairs, as at present established, is built up purposely to exclude the careless and happy soul.
>
> — Hawthorne

Young as you may be and new to the gay world as you may be, some legal matters call for long-range consideration. And the older you are the more important they become, especially if you have a lover.

Life insurance

To purchase an insurance policy you must have what is called an insurable interest in another person's longevity. Despite all we know of straight marriages, husbands and wives are considered to have such an interest in each other's lives. Gay couples are not. But there are ways around this.

You can, for instance, buy a policy on your own life and name your lover as the beneficiary of that policy. But this gets tricky: insurance companies are not obliged to sell insurance to anyone and traditionally they have refused to issue policies to identifiably homosexual persons. So, if you name your lover as beneficiary right off, you might be rejected. Designate a parent or some other relative as beneficiary until the policy becomes non-cancellable. Then you can change the name of the beneficiary to anyone you please.

You can buy an insurance policy on your lover's life if you and he are in business together. In that case the law agrees that each of you has an insurable interest in the life of the other. The idea is that the insurance gives the surviving business partner the funds to buy the other's share of the business from his heirs. Even in this case it is wise to keep the insurance company in the dark about your lives outside of the business partnership.

There is another way to solve this problem: the will.

Wills and inheritance

Most of us do not like to contemplate our death or the demise of anyone close to us. We often put off thinking about it to some later day. Most of us can expect to live for a long time, but life is full of surprises.

We do not have the rights that heterosexuals are granted by the legal relationship of marriage. Though this institution is denied to us, there is a good legal substitute for it. This is the will, which gives us the right to distribute our property as we see fit, to a lover or close friend, say, rather than an unsympathetic family.

Though not all relatives are boors, remember this: laws of inheritance vary from state to state, but in every one of them a person who dies without a will automatically makes his closest relation his heir. This can be somebody quite remote, a distant cousin or the like, but it will be a person related by blood or marriage. And if no relative can be found, the property will go to the state.

Many people say they have no property to speak of, so they won't bother with a will. They are likely to be mistaken. Anyone who contributes to a retirement plan at work probably has a death benefit which could amount to a good deal of money. Via automobile associations and certain other organizations there may be accidental death insurance that the owner is not even aware of.

Even if you only have the things you own with your lover or roommate, you'll probably want him to inherit your share of them, and the only way to do this is through a will.

And if you do want certain relatives to have your estate, a

will is still a good idea. A friend of ours was horrified to learn that under the laws of his state his property would not go to his brother as he had assumed, but to his parents from whom he had been estranged for many years and who had disinherited him.

A will is an excellent means of getting life insurance for your lover with perfect discretion. On any policy you merely name the beneficiary as "my estate," and the will does the rest.

Holographic wills. These are written by hand. They may have their uses in very uncomplicated situations or as a stopgap until you can get in to see a lawyer. Legally speaking, they are only slightly better than nothing. Many states do not recognize their validity, and where surviving relatives feel the estate is worth a court battle this sort of will provides pretty shaky protection for its maker's wishes.

If you do decide to write out your own will, be sure the holographic variety is legal not only in your state but also in any other state where you have property. Write it all yourself, entirely by hand, on blank paper, in ink. Do not type anything, and do not use any kind of printed form. Keep the text as clear and simple as you can. You're asking for trouble if you go much beyond something like "In the event of my death I leave all my property to my friend, John Smith." Sign and date the will at the bottom of the page. It does not have to be witnessed or notarized.

Seal the will in an envelope, and put it where it can be found easily: give it to a trusted friend, put it in a safe deposit box, or keep it at home in a place where your friends can locate it.

Formal wills. You could fake one up, and some people do, but a will is a tricky matter. A formal will should be prepared by a lawyer.

The cost of having a will drawn up for you can be a significant one, but ordinarily this is a one-shot deal. Minor changes are made by means of codicils to the will. They are simple and inexpensive; after the lawyer has made the first one you can probably use it as a model to do any others yourself. You don't have to make another will every time you split up with a lover.

In deciding the fate of your property you have a wide range of possibilities. For some men a simple will may do. For others, especially older couples who are comfortably fixed, the relatively complicated but exceedingly useful trust will may be the wisest choice.

The attorney is going to have to know a good deal about you in order not only to make the will but also to decide if a will contest should be anticipated. So if your family does not approve either of your way of life or of your associates, say so. Though you don't have to come right out and announce you're gay, it will help if you can do so. Even if you don't, the attorney will understand the situation unless he or she is exceedingly naive (not a common attribute of lawyers) and will adjust matters accordingly in the will.

Disinheriting. You have the legal right to disinherit your family if you wish. And the relatives can contest the will. Generally, there are three main attacks. First, the family can try to show that your mind was unsound, or that you were subject to the undue influence of another person, your male lover for instance. Second, they can attempt to prove that your failure to provide for them was unintentional. Third, your relatives can keep your will out of probate if it was not properly executed.

For the last two possibilities the best defense is to have a lawyer prepare the will. For the first, the younger you are when you make the will the better. If you're eighty in the shade, a little forgetful, perhaps aware that you're terminally ill, your wishes can be challenged with less difficulty.

As you can disinherit your family, your family can disinherit you, and you can contest their wills on the same grounds they can contest yours. Even if you can prove that you have been left out of the will merely and solely because you are gay, that's no help in court. If you can't prove that Dad was gaga when he made his will, or forgot to include you, or made it incorrectly, then there's nothing you can do about being disinherited.

In short, a well-drawn will can be capricious, unfair, vindictive, mean-spirited, or a form of punishment and still be perfectly legal. Anyone who is gay and in line for a significant inheritance may want to take this into consideration in deciding how open to be about his sex life.

Bequests can even be made on the condition that the beneficiary marry or produce children. That is, Grandma from her tomb can try to force you to go straight. (Nobody, however, can leave a bequest on the condition that the recipient turn gay. The law is so very butch.)

Will readings. This formality, popular as it is with playwrights and script-writers, is not part of current probate practice in the United States. So you have no reason to be apprehensive about being summoned to some lawyer's gloomy chambers to be reunited with relatives you detest and to hear a final denunciation of you and your way of life from the great beyond.

Alternatives to wills. There are several possibilities, but they all have drawbacks.

Joint tenancy. This allows two people to hold title to property so that if one dies the other becomes sole owner. Some books recommend this to gay people as a routine form of ownership. However, if the parties have a falling-out they may no longer desire that the survivor get the property. We think it is preferable for gay partners to hold title as tenants in common. Then each can dispose of his interest in the property by means of a will.

Some couples choose joint tenancy because they believe this is a way to avoid death taxes. Nope. The value of a deceased person's interest in the joint tenancy property is included in his estate for tax purposes.

Life insurance. Insurance proceeds can alleviate financial hardship for a surviving lover, but it does not transfer the interest in mutually owned goods, furnishings and the like. That requires a will.

Adoption. In some states one adult can adopt another so that the "parent" and "child" can inherit from each other. Sounds cozy, and it's been done by some well-known people. But there's one horrible problem: should the relationship go sour, and this does happen even after many years of closeness, it cannot be altered. There is no way in the law to un-adopt a child or to dump a parent. Thus, a man can end up stuck with onerous legal responsibilities for someone he can't stand and who loathes him.

Funeral instructions. Normally the relatives of a deceased person have the legal right to claim his body. In many instances vindictive or bigoted families have excluded a man's lover and friends from participating in the funeral arrangements or even from attending the services.

That's why written instructions are a good idea. While they are not necessarily legally binding they can greatly strengthen a lover's or friend's position when dealing with snarling relatives. The instructions frequently are included in wills, or they can be written separately. If you firmly state that such-and-such a person is to have charge of the funeral arrangements, most funeral directors will go along rather than risk a lawsuit. The more specific you are in your wishes, the harder it will be for the family to disregard them, and that holds even in states where such instructions do not have the strength of law.

If you wish to donate organs for transplants or leave your body to a medical school, don't merely request this in your instructions. Find out the required procedure, get the necessary papers, and carefully comply with the rules of your state in this matter.

Illnesses and Accidents. If a man becomes incapacitated his lover or friend, however close, has no legal authority to assume management of the unfortunate's affairs. As in the case of Kevin and Charles mentioned in the last chapter, the family has the right to take over, even if it is hostile, with greedy, homophobic brother Snotley in control. And if there is no family, then the government will step in.

In these circumstances a will is no help. Charles and Kevin should have kept their finances in order all along, and they could have taken either of two steps.

One thing they might have done was for each to nominate

the other as the conservator of his property in the event of incapacity. Even in states where the law allows this, the nomination may not be binding. But the courts will find it highly persuasive. Had this been arranged between our victimized pair of lovers, it would not have absolutely kept Snotley out of the picture. However, Charles' family would have to prove in court that valid reasons existed for disregarding Charles' choice of Kevin as his conservator.

The form for nomination of conservator should be drawn up by a lawyer.

The other step that Kevin and Charles might have taken would have been to execute powers of attorney for each other. A power of attorney is an authorization that one person gives to another to act in his behalf in legal and financial matters. There are two kinds, the special power, applying only to a specific matter or piece of property, and the general power, which is quite broad.

Neither kind of power of attorney should be granted lightly. Victimization is very easy. Only people who have a stable, trusting relationship with each other should even consider such a step.

Though you can get the forms at stationery stores and sign them in front of a notary, before you execute a power of attorney it's good to discuss the situation with a lawyer.

Couples who have a lot to protect might consider arranging both a nomination of conservator and a power of attorney, each for the other.

As a man who is new to gay life, you will not immediately encounter all the complications and problems discussed in these three legal chapters. Eventually though, the odds are that you will experience most of them. You will insure yourself against all sorts of grief and frustration if you get the proper advice when you need it, and then take the correct action. Remember, in the long run lawyers make a lot more money off people who screw things up than from people who do things right.

18 Gays & Professionals

We can be knowledgeable with other men's knowledge. . . .
— Montaigne

Much as gay people may need the services of a professional from time to time, we sometimes hesitate to seek the proper assistance out of fear — of exposure, misunderstanding, lack of sympathy, or outright rejection. In truth, though, we can usually avoid problems with a certain amount of care.

Doctors

While general practitioners are the rule in small towns and are making something of a comeback in urban areas, most physicians in cities are specialized. Because gay men are particularly exposed to sexually transmitted disorders, which are usually the concern of internal medicine, many of us choose internists as our regular physicians.

Whatever doctor you consult, he or she should have two qualifications. The first is a good up-to-date knowledge of gay medicine. Unfortunately, this subject is usually ignored in medical education and literature both. For example, *The Merck Manual*, a standard medical reference found in every doctor's office, mentions male rectal gonorrhea only in its more recent editions. And the intestinal parasites which are epidemic among gay men in the larger cities are regarded by many physicians as exotic afflictions, found only in people who have been traveling in the tropics.

Second, you must be able to be completely frank with the doctor about any activities that may have brought on your problem. Otherwise you run the risk of receiving inappropriate, ineffective treatment.

Obviously then, a gay doctor is best for a gay man, not only in terms of specialized knowledge and ease of communication but also for the sake of discretion. While no ethical physician will betray your confidence, other staff members can see your records, and should they contain information that would make for hot gossip in your neighborhood or all over a small town, well.... Even where men are open about their gayness and where residence in a large city provides anonymity, the gay doctor is likely to go to special efforts to keep records inaccessible to others. On one occasion a friend of ours had to get an injection, to be given by an assistant, in his internist's office. The aide studied the chart for a while, then said, "I can't figure out what the doctor's treating you for." That's discretion.

A gay physician is not an absolute necessity, and there may not be one where you live, but the doctor you do consult must be able to hear all you must say without going into shock or sending you out the door untreated.

Lawyers

Following the lead of the medical profession, attorneys in recent years have begun to specialize. And those who haven't are likely to fall into one of two broad categories: those lawyers who spend a lot of time in court and those who work in their offices. The first classification divides again into lawyers who handle criminal cases and those who deal with civil matters. In smaller population centers, though, many attorneys will still take on just about everything, with trial lawyers managing both civil and criminal cases.

Ordinarily a lawyer's client does not have to discuss his intimate life in order to get his legal work taken care of, so a straight lawyer will serve as well as a gay one. The only exceptions occur when a man is charged with some kind of illicit sexual activity, or possibly in a gay rights situation.

Of course a gay lawyer does have certain advantages. He or she may frame court documents so that they meet legal requirements without advertising to all the world that you are suing your ex-lover. And you can discuss freely with a gay lawyer just why you want to cut your family out of your will and leave everything to an unrelated male.

In recent years, at least in the larger cities, some lawyers have begun to gear their practices to the specific needs of a gay clientele. No single attorney, though, at least outside small towns, should be expected to handle everything. A specialist in criminal law should be consulted if you get busted. When a will or an agreement, a partnership or contract is needed, the lawyer who conducts an office practice is the one to see. And if you must sue that fatally charming young friend who won't repay the loan you foolishly made to him, you need a lawyer with experience in civil suits.

Remember that any one attorney may see the solution to your legal problems in terms of his or her own specialty. So, if you've only had dealings with an office practitioner, and you feel this new problem requires not merely a series of threatening letters but a fullblown lawsuit, ask for a referral to a specialist in litigation.

In terms of the law, two situations might require special precautions. Any gay man who likes sex in dangerous places should memorize the name and phone number of a good criminal lawyer. (Just as fellow inmates of a jail are lousy sources of legal advice, they are also very poor appraisers of lawyers' abilities.)

The highly closeted gay man who does not live in a large city might want to consult a lawyer outside his area, someone located in a place whose inhabitants are plugged into a separate cocktail-party circuit.

Legal fees. Uncomfortable as clients often feel about bringing up the subject of costs, reputable lawyers prefer to reach an understanding about their fees before any work is done, thus avoiding possible unpleasantness afterwards.

A consultation is the usual first step so the attorney can

determine what has to be done. As a rule a flat fee is charged for a consultation of a given length of time. Ask what it is before you see a lawyer, and if it sounds like too much, shop around.

Then, if the work is pretty much standardized, such as the preparation of a simple will, a set price will be quoted. Where the amount of time involved to do a legal job is not so predictable, an hourly rate will be charged. In criminal matters attorneys often quote a flat fee up through a specified point in the proceeding (through the preliminary hearing, for example), then charge so much per day for trial.

The important thing to remember is to talk about price *first*. If the lawyer strikes you as evasive or unnecessarily vague, go see another one.

Alternatives. You don't always need to consult a private lawyer for every legal problem. Where a criminal charge is made, the public defender's office will provide a defense lawyer. He or she may be as capable as anyone; this depends on how well the department is funded.

Wholly or partially subsidized by public funds, community or neighborhood legal service centers exist in many areas. Most of them are located in cities, but some exist in rural settings as well. Often these services specialize in assisting tenants, so they can give excellent advice about a lease (*before* you sign it) or when there is a dispute with a landlord. As a rule though, the staff is not prepared to draw up agreements or wills for people.

Other professionals

In dealing with accountants, insurance agents, real estate brokers and such, you need not reveal that you are gay. However, it will be to your advantage if you can be frank about where you are coming from and clear as to just how any certain other man is related to your life. Tax breaks for married couples will never help you. Your accountant will have to find other loopholes for your benefit. An insurance agent can help you get around the reluctance of many carriers to sell life insurance to homosexuals. A real estate salesman will know better than to show you crackerboxes in some suburb populated entirely by straight families and may be able to steer you to a lender who has no objection to financing a purchase by a same-sex couple.

Any professional's understanding and helpfulness is likely to be greatest if he too is gay.

Finding the right professional. The best way is probably the easiest: ask a gay friend to recommend somebody whose work he likes. If you get no help, try a gay businessman whom you know. If the owner of your favorite bar is gay, he is likely to have an accountant and a lawyer who are gay or at least not unsympathetic to homosexuals. And one professional is a good source of recommendation to another. Your gay lawyer may know a gay doctor. There are associations of professionals in major cities, listed in local gay directories or reachable through the local gay switchboard, information line, or counseling center.

Now that doctors and lawyers are permitted to advertise, you may find their announcements in local gay publications along with those of other professionals. They are likely to be homosexual, but that is not inevitable. And remember that a handsome display ad in a newspaper is not a certificate of competence.

In any good-sized city you should have little difficulty finding sympathetic professional assistance, but if you live in a small town or thinly populated area you may well have some problems. However, only your doctor must be close at hand. With other professionals, once you have established your relationship, face-to-face meetings are rarely necessary thereafter. Most matters can be taken care of by mail and telephone. Anyway, a gay man who dwells in suburbia or Dullsville is likely to make at least an occasional visit to the nearest big city; at these times a few minutes can be scheduled for such professional assistance as may be needed.

Evaluating competence

The very ignorance that requires us to employ professionals makes it difficult for us to judge the quality of their work. But there are some ways to decide whether a particular individual is likely to be doing a good job:

1. A competent man has satisfied clients who recommend him.
2. On subjects of general knowledge, can he respond in a reasonably intelligent manner? If he sounds stupid in conversation he may not be such a red-hot in his own field either.
3. Does he seem genuinely interested in you and your problems, or do you feel he's just trying to score his fee and get you out the door as quickly as possible? You do have to be realistic in assessing this; what professionals are selling is their time, so they can't spend all of it on you. And you are wise not to judge solely by a slick manner. Mere charm (or its lack) has no necessary relationship to ability.

As must be more than clear by now, nearly all institutions function to meet the needs of heterosexuals. As gays we are ignored. No account is taken of the fact that the sexual, legal, and social aspects of our lives often differ markedly from those of the straight majority. Given this situation we can easily find ourselves inconvenienced, shortchanged, treated with bias, or left unserved at all.

To redress the balance, to make the world function for us too, our best resource is to employ the skills of professionals whenever necessary. A great many heteros may be able to get from birth to death without concern for outside assistance. We cannot, except at the risk of imperiling the quality of our own lives and the well-being of those who mean the most to us.

19 <u>Gay Life Good & Bad</u>

There is no cure for birth and death save to enjoy the interval.

— Santayana

Out of necessity much in this book has dealt with the problems and difficulties of gay men's lives. In do doing we may have given you the impression that a homosexual experience has no advantages. This is far from true.

The majority of gay men can lead lives of great freedom and flexibility. Only a few of us have the responsibilities that go with family life. If you want to go from work to a movie, then pick up somebody in a bar and have sex, and finally arrive home after midnight, you can do so without creating panic and rancor in the suburbs. Should you want to leave town, make a radical change in your lifestyle or vocation, or set out traveling, no big problem. You can choose to work part-time and live poor in order to write novels or paint pictures or do nothing in particular.

Whatever you do for a living, you have more money for your own use out of your paycheck than does a married man with the same job. Usually the straight single male devotes a lot more cash and time to the process of getting laid than does his gay counterpart.

Sexually speaking, gay men are among the most liberated Americans. Unlike straight males, we are not limited to a few stereotypes. We can pick one role as most suitable, choosing from a wide selection; we can switch from one to another as mood suggests; we can even dream up something all our own.

In sexual knowledge and experience the average gay man is far ahead of his straight counterpart. By and large, homosexual men find the subject of sex neither frightening or nasty; talk of erotic matters is likely to be relaxed, amusing, and informative. Among heteros, though, notice how often the uptightness level rises when sex is discussed in any form except the dirty joke. These contrasting attitudes may stem largely from the fact that many straight males seem to feel their manhood is always slightly in question. Gay men need not be troubled by such unsureness. We do not, for instance, beat up straights in order to show how gay we are.

Social barriers that keep people in separate little boxes — race, class, religion, education, and so forth — certainly exist among gay men but generally are much weaker than among straights. As homosexuals we are not only all in the same boat but also likely to be all in the same bars, baths, and social gatherings. And sexual attraction makes rules that can strongly compete with those of society.

Since we are a percentage of the entire population, not merely from some small part of it, our diversity is great. In that, there is a great wealth of interest easily available to be enjoyed. To a considerable extent our friends can be whom we choose. We are not so enclosed by the family-school-job-neighborhood limitations that bore so many straights.

Our freedom enables us to indulge our tastes extensively in both the high and popular arts, where as patrons and also as practitioners our influence is considerable. It can be argued that neither classical ballet nor grand opera could survive without gay support. And the popular arts in the United States are dominated by three minority groups: blacks, the counterculture, and gay people.

On the other hand, our advantages exist only within narrow limits. These are defined by ourselves as well as others in the form of hatred. Within ourselves or out in society, this hatred is strong enough to force many of us to live our lives in secret.

We feel we cannot always depend on support from many

of society's institutions, particularly the police and the courts. Indeed, many of us cannot even be sure of the affections of our straight friends and closest kin.

And all too often we find it hard to even love and respect ourselves. Exposed from birth to society's negative views of homosexuality, many of us become victims of self-hatred.

As a man new to gay life who is probably right now in the process of reshaping his present and future, you should consider carefully both the positive and negative aspects of a gay existence. Much in the gay world is neutral in itself but, like money, can be used for good or ill. Your freedom and the limitations upon it both can be turned against you, and, impelled by self-hatred, the person most likely to do this is yourself.

You are a human being, after all, and your gayness is merely one of many attributes that you can claim. The wise gay man, however much or little he deals with the straight world, however much he drinks and dances and carries on, will cultivate a few deep, personally fulfilling pleasures, develop some solid personal interests, and have one or more satisfying long-term friendships.

As you look ahead you will also want to think about just how you wish to relate to the larger world. While many of us still hide some or all sides of our gay lives, this is increasingly less necessary. Partial and spotty as improvements have been, they have come about in recent years because many gay people have exerted great efforts to better our lot and get a fair shake from society.

Of course you can stay in the closet and go it alone. Many gay men do this, even when they have a choice in the matter. Against the advantages of passing as heterosexual in a mostly straight world, consider these drawbacks: When trouble comes the closeted gay is alone, without friends or allies. Nobody on his own can nourish such essentials as self-esteem, physical protection, and the respect (if not the love) of the society in which we must live.

The gay man who decides that he can come out pretty completely will find the gay world in the United States to be far more supportive today than it has ever been in the past. And the more of us who are upfront, the better for every one of us.

If that is not possible, a man can still join in a useful unity with fellow gays and not let the world know about it. If a man feels he can't march or picket or circulate petitions, or even sign them, in any effort there's always a lot of work behind the scenes. If you can't carry signs, you can still paint them. Anyone who is influential may be able to contribute a good deal by means of personal contacts. For true invisibility, nothing is more anonymous than supporting a boycott, and contributions by cash or postal money order are completely discreet.

Your life as a gay man may not be all that simple and easy, but it has its rewards, and like any existence it will be to a great extent what you make of it. And in these times of change your life could have an importance going beyond yourself. The patterns of living we gay men choose, the legal and political battles we fight, the unity or lack of it that we achieve, will all have a strong influence on gay men in the future. They, to a far greater extent than past generations, will have visible role models and a visible subculture.

By living as fully and as healthily as you can, you may very well help to diminish the problems of coming out and of living gay that most of us face now. You can demonstrate to those who are going to need to know it most that being a man who is gay gives no reason for either fear or shame.

Good luck. Have a good gay life.

Bibliography & Sources

Books on gay subjects have a long history. During much of that history they appeared only occasionally, usually to little notice and limited demand. In recent years, though, this trickle has turned into a flood. Old or new, some of the work is excellent, some silly, and a little is homophobia in respectable disguise. We have selected a bare minimum of titles, most of them well known among gay men, many of them distinguished, and all chosen because they illuminate various aspects of gay life. In addition we have listed other sources of information which may be useful.

Gay-oriented books and periodicals are not as hard to find as you may think. Specialized outlets are not their sole distributors. Many good owner-run bookstores carry them, as do some chain operations and many feminist and alternative-lifestyle bookshops. Leftist bookstores often have a shelf or two of gay books, and some adult bookstores may carry more than just erotic reading matter.

The *Gayellow Pages* lists bookstores city by city, both the regular kind and the x-rated places. *Bob Damron's Address Book* is useful too, though mostly for adult bookstores.

For the man who must buy his reading material through the mail, or who would rather do it that way, many gay-oriented bookstores offer mail order services and send catalogs. Sometimes these can be had for the asking, but usually there is a small charge. The following are some of the better known concerns that deal extensively, sometimes exclusively, with gay reading matter. Some of them may stock a certain amount of erotic material, but none of them is an adult bookstore.

Northeast

Oscar Wilde Memorial Bookshop, 15 Christopher Street, New York, New York 10014

Three Lives and Co., 131 Seventh Avenue South, New York, New York, 10014

The Elysian Fields, 81-13Y Broadway, Elmhurst, New York 11377 (mail order only)

Paths Untrodden Book Service, Box 459, Village Station, New York, New York 10014 (mail order only)

Giovanni's Room, 345 South Twelfth Street, Philadelphia, Pennsylvania 19107

Glad Day Book Shop, 43 Winter Street, Boston, Massachusetts 02108

Central

Category Six Books, 909 East Colfax, Denver, Colorado 80218

New Earth Books and Records, 24 East Thirty-ninth Street, Kansas City, Missouri 64111

Chosen Books, 940 West McNichols, Detroit, Michigan, 48203

A Room of One's Own Bookstore, 317 West Johnson Street, Madison, Wisconsin 53703

South

Lambda Rising, Inc., 2012 S Street NW, Washington, D.C. 20009

Books As Seeds, 200½ Andrew Jackson Way NE, Huntsville, Alabama 35801

Faubourg-Marigny Bookstore, 600 Frenchmen, New Orleans, Louisiana 70116

Christopher's Kind, 70 Thirteenth Street NE, Atlanta, Georgia 30309

Hobbit Habit, 146 East Clayton Street, Athens, Georgia 30601

Southwest
Wilde 'n' Stein, 802 Westheimer, Houston, Texas
    70066
Books Brothers, Ltd., 3242 East Speedway, Tucson,
    Arizona 85716

West Coast
A Different Light, 4014 Santa Monica Boulevard, Los
    Angeles, California 90029
Unicorn Bookstore, 8940 Santa Monica Boulevard, Los
    Angeles, California 90029
Walt Whitman Booksshop, 2319 Market Street, San
    Francisco, California 94114
A Different Drummer, 420 Broadway East, Seattle,
    Washington 98102

Canada
Glad Day Book Shop, 648A Yonge Street, Toronto,
    Ontario M4Y 2A6
Alternate Bookshop, 1588 Barrington Street (second
    floor), Mailing address: Box 276 Stn. M; Halifax,
    Nova Scotia B3J 2N7
Ariel Books, 2766 West Fourth Avenue, Vancouver,
    British Columbia V6K 1R1.

When you order any gay catalogue or book, or subscribe
to a gay periodical, it almost certainly will be sent in the
famous Plain Brown Wrapper.

Directories and Catalogues
Bob Damron's Address Book. Bob Damron. Published
annually. An extensive, annotated listing of gay bars, baths,
restaurants, adult bookstores, and cruising places, both in
the United States and Canada. The best bar guide. A single
shortcoming: no telephone numbers. Sold in gay oriented
bookstores and businesses, gay bars, and available from Bob
Damron Enterprises, Box 14-077, San Francisco, California
94114.

Gayellow Pages. Various authors. National and regional

editions, updated about twice a year. Not so useful for bars and baths as Damron's guide, but excellent for its wide coverage of gay organizations, services, and activities. Available at gay bookstores or from its publisher, Renaissance House, Box 292, Village Station, New York, New York 10014.

Colorful People and Places. Michael J. Smith. 1983. Quarterly Press. A guide for members of minority groups; lists bars, private clubs, organizations, magazines, and other resources.

Gay Source: A Catalog for Men. Dennis Sanders. 1977. Coward, McCann & Geohagan. Informative miscellany on matters of interest to gay men; a few sections have become dated.

A Gay Bibliography. The Gay Task Force of the American Library Association. 1980. Pamphlet listing numerous books and films on such subjects as religion, psychology, law, history, literature, and politics; also, periodicals, bibliographies, and directories. Order from the publisher, the American Library Association, Box 2383, Philadelphia, Pennsylvania 19103.

Homosexuality in Canada. Alex Spence. 1980. Pink Triangle Press. A useful bibliography.

Periodicals
Local, regional, and national, gay-oriented newspapers and magazines abound (as can be seen in *A Gay Bibliography*). A few are nationally distributed and well known:

The Advocate. A national gay magazine for news, the arts, and gay history; includes an extensive personal ad section. Newspaper format, issued every two weeks. Oriented toward the urban, younger, middle-class gay. Box 5847, San Mateo, California 94402.

Christopher Street. A monthly magazine, literary, humorous, with some discussion of serious gay issues. On slick paper. "The gay New Yorker." 249 West Broadway, New York, New York 10013.

Fag Rag. Twice a year. On newsprint. Radical-literary, oriented toward very young men and the counterculture. Box 331, Kenmore Station, Boston, Massachusetts 02215.

Gay Community News. A weekly newspaper. Good source of news on national gay rights battles. Some local emphasis as well. 167 Tremont Street, Boston, Massachusetts 02111.

Journal of Homosexuality. A quarterly. Scholarly articles by professionals, on social and legal matters. Haworth Press, 149 Fifth Avenue, New York, New York 10010.

RFD. A quarterly. For gay men living in rural areas. Route 1, Box 127E, Bakersville, North Carolina 27243.

The Body Politic. A newspaper. Ten issues a year. Canada's national news and literary paper. Box 7289, Station A, Toronto, Ontario, Canada M5W 1X9.

Background & History
Greek Homosexuality. K.J. Dover. 1978. Harvard University Press. A learned discussion of the beginnings of the western gay heritage.

Homosexuality — A History — from Ancient Greece to Gay Liberation. Vern L. Bullough. 1978. Meridian.

Christianity, Social Tolerance and Homosexuality: Gay People in Europe from the Beginning of the Christian Era to the Fourteenth Century. John Boswell. 1980. University of Chicago Press. Scholarly study of the varying degrees of acceptance of homosexuality in medieval Europe.

Gay American History: Lesbians and Gay Men in the U.S.A.; a Documentary. Edited by Jonathan Katz. 1976. Thomas Y. Crowell. A real eye-opener.

Out of the Closets: The Sociology of Homosexual Liberation. Laud Humphries. 1972. Prentice-Hall. A study of the growth of the American gay liberation struggle.

Fiction & Drama
The many novels, short stories, and plays on gay themes range from first-rate works of literature through beach

blanket reading to hardcore porno. These are two good guides through the library stacks and bookstore shelves:

Playing the Game — The Homosexual Novel in America. Roger Austen. 1977. Bobbs-Merrill. Fine history and guide.

The Male Homosexual in Literature: A Bibliography. Ian Young. 1975. Scarecrow Press. Four commentaries and thousands of listings.

CHAPTER 1 — Coming Out

Most books that explain the life-ways of gay people are directed toward the heterosexual reader, but many will be informative for anyone new to gay life. These books are often available in public libraries, and most of them have been reprinted in inexpensive paperback editions.

These are some of the best general coverage books:

Familiar Faces, Hidden Lives — The Story of Homosexual Men in America Today. Howard Brown, M.D. 1976. Harcourt Brace Jovanovich. Good common-sense approach; much of special interest to men in professions.

The Homosexual in America — A Subjective Approach. Donald Webster Cory. 1951. Greenberg. The pioneering effort. Much of course is historical now, but a lot still applies.

The Gay Mystique — the Myth and Reality of Male Homosexuality. Peter Fisher. 1972. Stein & Day. A good survey of gay ways and institutions.

Books more directly concerned with the experience of coming out include a number of contemporary novels. However, the requirements of storytelling can distort realities toward pure delight, or, more often, grim horror. Older fiction is even less useful, with gay existence leading to such unlikely fates as a lifetime of celibate loneliness, conversion to heterosexuality, a plunge into madness, or an untimely and often gruesome death by murder or suicide. The very old novels are often quite vague and must be read between the lines. For the experience of coming out, more solid information is found in nonfiction. These are some of the better examples:

Word is Out: Stories of Some of Our Lives. Nancy Adair and Casey Adair. 1978. New Glide Publications. Twenty-six gay men and lesbians from widely varying backgrounds tell about their lives, including many descriptions of the experience of coming out. Informative, funny, poignant. This book was made from the excellent color film of the same title, which in long and short versions can be rented from New Yorker Films, 16 West Sixty-first Street, New York, New York 10023.

With Downcast Gays — Aspects of Homosexual Self-Oppression. Andrew Hodges and David Hutter. Pink Triangle Press. 1977. Thought-provoking essay exploring often unrecognized manifestations of gay self-hatred. Includes a very good discussion on liberal "tolerance" of gays as masked homophobia.

Under the Rainbow — Growing Up Gay. Arnie Kantrowitz. 1977. William Morrow. A nice Jewish boy goes through hell, high water, and gay liberation, saved by intelligence and a great sense of humor.

The Best Little Boy in the World. John Reid. 1973. G.P. Putnam's Sons. Amusingly recounted experiences of a Northeastern preppie, who candidly reveals he's still in the process of figuring out how to handle gay relationships.

Society and the Healthy Homosexual. George Weinberg. 1972. St. Martin's Press. A sympathetic straight psychotherapist writes on anti-gay bias in psychoanalysis, the negative aspects of aversion therapy, and discusses very helpfully the problems involved in telling one's parents.

These are two good books for parents of gays:

Now that You Know. Betty Fairchild and Nancy Hayward. 1979. Harcourt Brace Jovanovich.

A Family Matter: A Parent's Guide to Homosexuality. Dr. Charles Silverstein. 1977. McGraw-Hill.

CHAPTER 2 — The Bars

Many of the books that discuss the gay world have a chapter or two on bars, but otherwise this milieu has not been covered to any great extent. One exception is *Other Voices — The Style of a Male Homosexual Tavern* by Kenneth E. Read and published in 1980 by Chandler & Sharp. It is a fascinating anthropological study, but the bar it examines is a real dive and not typical of most gay drinking places.

Otherwise, the best books to consult are those listed at the beginning of the Chapter 1 section.

CHAPTER 3 — The Baths

Again, most of the general books on gay life have discussions of bath houses. See also *The Advocate Guide to Gay Health*, listed in the Chapter 13-14 section of this bibliography.

CHAPTER 4 — Cruising Places

Tearoom Trade: Impersonal Sex in Public Places. Laud Humphreys. 1975. Aldine. A detailed sociological study that serves as an excellent how-to-do-it guide.

The Gay Mystique — the Myth and Reality of Male Homosexuality, listed as a reference in the Chapter 1 section of this bibliography, is the source of the quotation.

CHAPTER 5 — Prostitution

Midnight Cowboy. James Leo Herlihy. 1965. Simon and Schuster. Well-known novel of street hustlers in New York City.

For Money or Love: Boy Prostitution in America. Robin Lloyd. 1976. Vanguard. A straight journalist's rather emotional investigation.

City of Night. John Rechy. 1963. Grove Press. Novel of street hustlers in Los Angeles.

CHAPTER 6 — New Alternatives

Check the directories and guidebooks listed at the beginning of this bibliography. Read local publications.

CHAPTER 7 — First Experience &
CHAPTER 8 — First Love

Sex in Society. Alex Comfort. 1975. Citadel. Not specifically gay in content but interesting for its view of the role of sex in our world; source of the quotation.

Loving Men — A Photographic Guide to Gay Male Love-making. Mark Freedman and Harvey Mayes. 1976. Hark. A sex manual which emphasizes the psychology of successful cruising and lovemaking.

The Joy of Gay Sex: An Intimate Guide for Gay Men to the Pleasures of a Gay Lifestyle Dr. Charles Silverstein and Edmund White. 1977. Crown. Not limited to sexual techniques; it has comments on many aspects of gay life. Nice illustrations.

Men Loving Men. Mitch Walker. 1977. Gay Sunshine Press. Photographs, good suggestions; new-consciousness approach

CHAPTER 9 — The Older Gay Man

"Adjustments to Aging Among Gay Men," by Douglas C. Kimmel, in *Positively Gay,* listed as a reference in the Chapter 13-14 section of this bibliography.

"Age," in *Male Homosexuals — their Problems and Adaptations.* Martin S. Weinberg and Colin J. Williams. 1974. Oxford University Press. A good discussion of the lives of older gay men; source of the quotation.

Looking Good: A Guide for Men. Charles Hix. 1977. Hawthorn Books.

Dressing Right: A Guide for Men. Charles Hix with Brian Burdine. 1978. St. Martin's Press.

Exercise in the Office — Easy Ways to Better Health and Firmer Figures. Robert R. Spackman, Jr. 1968. Southern Illinois University Press.

Isometric Exercises for Figure Improvement and Body Conditioning. Earl L. Wallis and Gene A. Logan. 1964. Prentice-Hall.

Beauty by Design: A Complete Look at Cosmetic Surgery. Kurt J. Wagner, M.D. and Gerald Imber, M.D. 1979. McGraw-Hill.

CHAPTER 10 — The Underage Gay

Reflections of a Rock Lobster: A Story About Growing Up Gay. Aaron Fricke. 1981. Alyson. Autobiography of a young gay man who came out in a big way when he invited another male to be his date at his high school's senior prom.

A Way of Life, A Way of Love — A Young Person's Introduction to What it Means to Be Gay. Frances Hanckel and John Cunningham. 1979. Lothrop, Lee & Shephard. Sympathetic and helpful but heavier on advice than information.

Men's Lives: A Documentary Film About Masculinity in America. Josh Honig and Will Roberts. 1974. In color. Rental from New Day Films, Box 315, Franklin Lakes, New Jersey 07417. Not specifically gay-oriented, but shows clearly the pressures that form male role-patterns in childhood including, implicitly, homophobia. Interesting and humorous.

The Rights of Young People. Alan N. Sussman. 1977. Discus/Avon Books. This American Civil Liberties Union Handbook is not gay-oriented, but is full of such useful information as the age of majority for each state, legal age for buying liquor, receiving pornographic materials, and obtaining medical treatment without parental consent. A good discussion of juvenile court powers and procedures, including the rights of underage persons.

Young, Gay & Proud! Sasha Alyson and others. 1980.

Alyson. Personal experiences, telling others, meeting other young gays, health care. Very positive viewpoint.

Youth Liberation. This now-defunct organization published a number of pamphlets about young people's rights. Three of them are now distributed by Carrier Pigeon, PO Box 2783, Boston, MA 02208. They are: Student and Youth Organizing ($3.00); Young People and the Law ($3.00) and Children's Rights Handbook ($4.00). Prices are postpaid.

CHAPTER 11 — The Gay Minorities

S & M

Good though brief discussions will be found in books listed elsewhere in this bibliography, in *The Gay Mystique* (see the Chapter 1 section), *Gay Source* (see the General section), and in *The Joy of Gay Sex* (see the Chapter 7-8 section).

"Inside Sado/Masochism" by Ian Young in *The New Gay Liberation Book: Writings and Photographs on Gay (Men's) Liberation.* Len Richmond and Gary Noguera, editors. 1979. Ramparts Press.

Leatherman's Handbook II. Larry Townsend. 1983. Modernismo. Available in some adult bookstores, shops in leather bars, and from the author at 525 North Laurel, Los Angeles, California 90048. Between stretches of nice pornography and dubious sociology the author gives much information and background.

A complete handkerchief color-code chart appears in *Bob Damron's Address Book* (listed in the Directories and Catalogues section).

Transvestism

Dressing Up — Transvestism and Drag: The History of an Obsession. Peter Ackroyd. 1979. Simon & Schuster. A short history of cross-dressing, with many illustrations and some interesting speculations.

How to Be a Woman — Though Male. Virginia Charles Prince 1971. Chevalier. A how-to-do-it book on dressing and grooming for female impersonation.

Female Impersonator News. Claims to be "the only drag newspaper." News, advice, erotic fiction, personal ads, frank photos. Neptune Productions, Box 360, Belmar, New Jersey 07719.

Effeminates

The Naked Civil Servant. Quentin Crisp. 1977. Holt, Rinehart & Winston. The good and bad sides of the life of a delightful Englishman who is a classic nelly queen.

Boy Lovers

Sexual Experience Between Men and Boys — Exploring the Pederast Underground. Parker Rossman. 1976. Association Press. A psychological and sociological study, detached but sympathetic.

The Age Taboo: Gay Male Sexuality, Power and Consent. Daniel Tsang, Editor. 1981. Alyson. A collection of recent writings on man/boy love from various, mostly radical, points of view.

North American Man/Boy Love Association (NAMBLA). An activist organization with publications, conferences, prisoner support, and local chapters with meetings (mostly in the Northeast). Box 1740, Midtown Station, New York, New York 10018.

CHAPTER 12 — Employment

The legal problems of gays in terms of jobs and occupational licenses are discussed in *The Rights of Gay People* (see the Chapters 15-17 section).

The National Gay Task Force, 80 Fifth Avenue, New York, New York 10010, has a number of pamphlets dealing with employment, particularly *The NGTF Corporate Survey* on hiring policies in relation to gays. and *Professional Gay Caucus List.*

CHAPTER 13 — Medical Problems &
CHAPTER 14 — Recreational Drug Use

Old medical books, especially "doctor books" and similar manuals for home treatment, often take the attitude that sex is in general a dangerous, debilitating activity, and that gay sex is degenerate, at best. For any medical question get your information from the newest sources.

The Advocate Guide to Gay Health. R. Fenwick. 1978, 1982. Alyson.

Gay Health Guide. Robert Rowan and Paul Gillette. 1978. Little, Brown.

Positively Gay — New Approaches in Gay Life. Betty Berzon and Robert Leighton, editors. 1979. Celestial Arts. Essays on gay life; the slant is psychological with emphasis on a liberated gay identity.

The National Gay Health Directory. Annual edition. Available from the National Gay Health Coalition Educational Foundation, Box 677, Old Chelsea Station, New York, New York 10011. A list of health services, gay-sponsored or not, that are available to gay men and lesbians. Includes Canada.

The New Venereal Disease Prevention for Everyone. Written and published by the American Foundation for the Prevention of VD, Inc., 335 Broadway, New York, New York 10013. A very helpful pamphlet on sexual hygiene. Copies are available for a tax-deductible contribution, in Spanish and French as well as in English (Portions of the text are printed from time to time in gay periodicals.)

Pro kits. Sanitubes can be ordered retail from the Sanitube Company, Mount Kisco, New York 10549, if you can't find them locally. The Reese Chemical Company will do the same if it can't give you the name of a nearby pharmacy that sells their product, the Doughboy Prophylactic. Write to Reese Chemical Company, 10716 First Avenue, Cleveland, Ohio 44106.

VD Hotline. A national referral information service, run by volunteers. Not specifically gay, but usually there is a gay person to talk with. The line is in service from 8:30 a.m. to 10:30 p.m., Pacific Coast time. The national number is (800) 227-8922; in California it's (800) 982-5883

CHAPTERS 15-17 — Gay Men and The Law

The Rights of Gay People. E. Carrington Boggan, Marilyn G. Haft, Charles Lister, and John P. Rupp. 1975. Avon/Discus. This American Civil Liberties Union handbook is dated in some respects, not lively reading, but full of useful information on the problems gays may encounter in employment, the armed forces, with security clearances, housing, and child custody.

A Legal Guide for Lesbian and Gay Couples. Hayden Curry and Denis Clifford. 1980. Addison-Wesley. Extended discussions of legal subjects which we have covered only briefly. Various instructions and agreement forms. (We feel it's too risky, though, to follow their suggestion to make your own formal will.)

Martindale-Hubbell Law Directory. Annual. Martindale-Hubbell, Inc. A state by state list of lawyers and law summary, this is where you can find out if holographic wills are valid in your state. Commonly available in public library reference collections.

Self-Defense — A Basic Course. Bruce Tegnér. 1979. Thor Publishing Written for men who are not practiced in defending themselves, this explains "techniques using the least possible force."

Everybody's Guide to Small Claims Court. Ralph Warner. 1979. Nolo Press. Not gay-oriented but helpful in determining if a court action against a roommate, landlord, or merchant is worth the trouble. Detailed instructions for filing a small claims suit.

CHAPTER 19 — Gay Life Good and Bad

Who Happen to Be Gay. A color film produced and directed by Dale Beldin and Mark Krenzien. 1979. Rental from Direct Cinema Limited Library, Box 315, Franklin Lakes, New Jersey 07417. Six openly gay professionals discuss their lives and why they choose not to hide their sexual preference. Well done, upbeat documentary.

National Gay Task Force, 80 Fifth Avenue, New York, New York 10010. This organization works to promote civil rights for gay people throughout the United States, and it offers a series of informative, inexpensive pamphlets on gay problems.

You'll also enjoy these other Alyson books

Don't miss our FREE BOOK offer on the last page.

REFLECTIONS OF A ROCK LOBSTER
A story about growing up gay
by Aaron Fricke; $4.95

No one in Cumberland, Rhode Island was surprised when Aaron Fricke showed up at his high school prom with a male date; he had sued his school for the right to do so, and the papers had been full of the news ever since. Yet until his senior year, there would have been nothing to distinguish Aaron Fricke from anyone else his age. You'd never have guessed he was gay — and Aaron did his best to keep it that way. He created a shell around himself as protection against a world that he knew would reject him if it knew the truth. But finally his anger became too great, and he decided to make a stand.

Now, in *Reflections of a Rock Lobster*, you can read Fricke's moving story about growing up gay — about coming to terms with being different, and a lesson in what gay pride can really mean in a small New England town.

YOUNG, GAY AND PROUD!
edited by Sasha Alyson; $2.95

One high school student in ten is gay. Here is the first book ever to address the problems and needs of that often-invisible minority. It helps young people deal with questions like: Am I really gay? What would my friends think if I told them? Should I tell my parents? Does anybody else feel the way I do?

THE MEN WITH THE PINK TRIANGLE
by Heinz Heger, $4.95

Here is the true story of a chapter in gay history that has long been hidden from view. In 1939, the author was a young medical student, in love with the son of a Nazi officer. In March of that year the Gestapo abruptly arrested him for homosexuality, and he spent the next six years in concentration camps. Like thousands of other homosexuals, he was forced to wear a pink triangle on his shirt so he could be readily identified for special abuses.

Richard Hall, book columnist for *The Advocate*, praised this as "One of the ten best books of the year" and *Gay Community News* warns that "You may find yourself riveted to your seat" by Heger's narrative.

THE SPARTAN
by Don Harrison, $5.95

Pantarkes' goal is to enter the Olympics and win the laurel crown. But at the age of 16, after accidentally killing the son of a high official, Pantarkes is forced to flee his home in

Sparta. For two years his Olympic dreams are postponed as he is drafted into the Theban army to help fight against the invading Macedonians; then finds himself in the middle of a revolt against the Spartan tyrants who had earlier forced him to flee.

This brisk-paced novel provides a vivid picture of classical Greece and the early Olympics, and of an era when gay relationships were a common and valued part of life

THE ADVOCATE GUIDE TO GAY HEALTH
R. D. Fenwick; $6.95

You'd expect a good gay health book to cover a wide range of information, and this one does. What you wouldn't expect is that it could be so enjoyable to read! Here you'll find the expected information about sexually-transmitted diseases; you'll also learn about such things as what you should know before going into sex therapy; how some lesbians and gay men have handled their fear about aging; and the important lessons of the holistic health movement.

a novel by James Barr
introduction by Samuel M. Steward

QUATREFOIL
by James Barr
introduction by Samuel Steward; $6.95

Phillip Froelich is in trouble. The year is 1946, and he's traveling to Seattle where he will face a court-martial for acting insubordinate to a lazy officer in the closing days of World War II. On the way to Seattle he meets Tim Danelaw, and soon the trial is among the least of Phillip's concerns...

So begins *Quatrefoil*, a novel originally published in 1950. It marked a milestone in gay writing, with two of the first non-stereotyped gay characters to appear in American fiction. For readers of the Fifties, it was a rare chance to counteract the negative imagery that surrounded them.

Now we have reissued *Quatrefoil*. Readers today will find that it provides a vivid picture of what it was like to be gay in our recent past; on top of that, it's still an entertaining and well-crafted novel

To get these books:

Ask at your favorite bookstore for the books listed here. You may also order by mail. Just fill out the coupon below, or use your own paper if you prefer not to cut up this book.

GET A FREE BOOK! When you order any three books listed here at the regular price, you may request a **free** copy of any book priced at $4.95 or less.

BOOKSTORES: Standard trade terms apply. Details and catalog available on request.

Send orders to: **Alyson Publications, Inc.**
　　　　　　　　PO Box 2783, Dept. B-21
　　　　　　　　Boston, MA 02208

— — — — — — — — — — — — — — — — —

Enclosed is $_____ for the following books. (Add $.75 postage when ordering just one book; if you order two or more, we'll pay the postage.)

☐ The Advocate Guide to Gay Health ($6.95)
☐ The Age Taboo ($5.95)
　　Essays from many perspectives about man/boy love
☐ Coming Out Right ($5.95)
☐ The Men With the Pink Triangle ($4.95)
☐ Quatrefoil ($6.95)
☐ Reflections of a Rock Lobster ($4.95)
☐ The Spartan ($5.95)
☐ Young, Gay and Proud! ($2.95)
☐ Send a free copy of _____ as
　　offered above. I have ordered at least three other books.

name: _____

address: _____

city: _____ state. _____ zip: _____

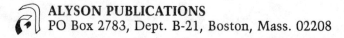

ALYSON PUBLICATIONS
PO Box 2783, Dept. B-21, Boston, Mass. 02208